THE

FAMILY NURSE;

OR

COMPANION OF
THE AMERICAN FRUGAL HOUSEWIFE.

BY MRS. CHILD,

Author of the "American Frugal Housewife,"
"Mother's Book," "Girl's Book," &c.

REVISED BY A MEMBER OF THE MASSACHUSETTS MEDICAL SOCIETY.

"How shall I cure Dyspepsia?"
"Live upon sixpence a day, and earn it."
Dr. Abernethy.

APPLEWOOD BOOKS
BEDFORD, MASSACHUSETTS

The Family Nurse was originally published by
Charles Hendee of Boston in 1837.

Thank you for purchasing an Applewood book.
Applewood reprints America's lively classics—
books from the past that are of interest to
modern readers. For a free copy of our
current catalog, write to: Applewood Books,
P.O. Box 365, Bedford, MA 01730.

ISBN 1-55709-461-6

10 9 8 7 6 5 4 3 2 1

Printed in the United States of America

Library of Congress Cataloging-in-Publication Data
Child, Lydia Maria Francis, 1802–1880.
    The family nurse, or Companion of the frugal
housewife / by Lydia Maria Child.
        p.   cm.
    Reprint. Originally published: Boston: C.J.
Hendee, 1837.
    ISBN 1-55709-461-6
    1. Home nursing.   2. Medicine, Popular.
I. Title.
RT61.C486   1997
610.73–dc21   97-84
                                           CIP

PREFACE.

THIS book merely contains the elements of nursing, and is by no means intended to supersede the advice of a physician. It is simply a household friend, which the inexperienced may consult on common occasions, or sudden emergencies, when medical advice is either unnecessary, or cannot be obtained.

Among the variety of books consulted for this purpose, those which have been most carefully examined are Dewees on the Diseases of Women ; Dewees on the Diseases of Children ; Bigelow's Medical Botany ; Thatcher's Modern Practice ; Thatcher's Dispensatory ; and Wood's and Bache's Dispensatory. From The Young Lady's Friend I have likewise taken many useful hints.

My own inexperience has been assisted by aged relatives and judicious nurses ; and every part of the work has been submitted to the examination of a member of the Massachusetts Medical Society, for several years a physician in active and successful practice in Boston. To him I am indebted for a very patient supervision and many valuable suggestions.

My strongest anxiety has been to make the book *safe* ; and whatever its demerits may be, I believe it contains no prescription that can endanger life or health, if a common degree of judgment be excercised.

In the diseases of children, I have almost uniformly followed Dr. Dewees, who is very celebrated in that branch of his profession ; but with regard to Croup, I took the advice of experienced physicians, who deemed his prescriptions too mild for a New England climate.

Calomel is never prescribed ; not on account of undue prejudice against a medicine highly useful on many occasions, but because it is considered unsafe when administered by inexperienced hands.

Tinctures are introduced sparingly and reluctantly. Though a convenient form of preserving some medicines, they may almost always be dispensed with, and the use of them frequently induces habits of intemperance.

Medical terms are sometimes used for the sake of brevity and convenience ; but at the end of the volume there is an explanation of them, in clear and simple language.

For many reasons, the preparation of this work has been an arduous and disagreeable task ; but the recollection of a verse learned in childhood has sometimes cheered me :—

> " Did I this day, for small or great,
> My own pursuits forego,
> To lighten, by a feather's weight,
> The mass of human woe ! "

Still I should take undue credit to myself if I professed that the usefulness of such a book was my strongest motive. If any other than very practical works would sell extensively, I fear I should still be lingering in more poetic regions.

This volume is very obviously not intended for the drawing-room. If written in language plain enough to be understood, it could not in the very nature of the subject, be otherwise than indelicate, in the world's estimation. Considerations of this nature induced me to lay it aside for a long time unfinished. This was the effect of false modesty. As the world becomes wiser and better, I trust the various functions of the human body will be spoken of with more philosophical purity, and regarded merely as temporary mediums for the growth of the soul.

[*Look at Note, page* 148.]

HINTS

FOR THE PRESERVATION OF HEALTH.

"An ounce of prevention is worth a pound of cure."

NEVER meddle with medicines, unless some disorder of the system renders them really necessary. Remember the friendly warning in the epitaph on an old gravestone : " I was well ; would be better ; took physic ; and here I am."

Observe the effects of particular articles on your system, and indulge or refrain accordingly. To preserve the digestive organs in good order, may almost be called the one thing needful, as it regards bodily health.

If not as well as usual, eat nothing ; fasting and cold water are the best physicians, nineteen times out of twenty.

Do not eat a variety of things at the same meal ; nor indulge merely for the pleasure of it, when the wants of nature are satisfied. Avoid rich and stimulating articles of food and drink.

Take your meals at regular hours.

Many think distilled liquors are necessary for those who work in cold, damp places ; but in fact they only increase the danger of taking cold. Their effects are evil continually.

Sleep in rooms with a free circulation of air. Have

no fire burning, or fragrant flowers in the room. Do not cover your face with the bed-clothes. Have clean bed linen once a week. Do not have a current of air blowing directly on your bed.

Feather beds are debilitating, except in the very coldest weather.

Rise early, and retire to rest in good season. Regularity in food and sleep is a great preservative of health.

Be not afraid of fatigue. That kind of exercise is best which employs body and mind. A walk in connection with active business, or to relieve the necessities of the destitute, is worth ten walks merely for exercise.

Very many humors and diseases originate in a want of personal cleanliness. Wash your whole person thoroughly, at least once or twice a week ; and rub yourself with a coarse crash towel, or brush, till the surface glows. This is particularly salutary for those who sew a good deal, or lead any kind of sedentary life. If done at night, it is apt to induce refreshing sleep. Many a consumption might be prevented by proper regard to this suggestion.

Those troubled with cold feet and a tendency of blood to the head, will find it an excellent remedy to dip their feet in cold water, as soon as they are out of bed, all the year round. The feet should be merely dipped, and *taken out instantly;* then rubbed with a coarse cloth, or brush, till they glow. None but very weakly people could possibly be injured by it.

Clean your teeth with a brush and cold water in the morning, and rinse them once or twice a day ; above all, have them clean when you go to bed, that they may not collect impurities during the night. To chew charcoal slowly once or twice a week, sweetens the breath, and tends to preserve the teeth from decay ; it will sometimes even arrest it when begun. To use it merely as a tooth powder is far less salutary. Tooth-picks, by keeping the teeth well separated and cleansed, help to preserve them. Metal ones are injurious; those made of quill are uncleanly, being commonly kept for some time; the best ones are made of willow, or some pliable wood,—they do not hurt the gums, and are thrown away when used. All substances very hot, or very cold, are hurtful to the teeth; likewise smoking and chewing tobacco; and too free use of very sweet articles, and excess of animal food.

The frequent use of a fine ivory comb is not good for the hair. It is better to wash the head often in cool water, and brush it very thoroughly. If the hair comes out very much, sea-water, or water with salt dissolved in it, is much recommended as a frequent bath. Cleanliness is good for the hair as well as for other parts of the body.

Wash the eyes thoroughly in cold water. Do not sew, or read, at twilight, or by too dazzling light. If far-sighted, read with rather less light, and with the book somewhat nearer to the eye, than you desire; if near-sighted, read with a book as far off as possible. Both these imperfections may be thus diminished.

If flannel has been worn on the throat, choose the morning of a mild day to remove it, and be careful about exposure to the cold for some days after.

If stockings and shoes get wet, change them. It is a mistaken idea that it is healthy to dry them on.

Be careful not to put on clothes before they are aired. Avoid sitting upon the damp ground, or sleeping in damp sheets.

A feather-bed is the safest place in a severe thunder storm. The middle of the room is a better seat than near windows, or fire-places. Metals attract lightning. Trees are an unsafe shelter.

After exposure to severe cold, do not suddenly approach a fire, or drink hot drinks; but acquire warmth very gradually.

If you find yourself seriously ill, send for a good physician—one who understands his trade.

HINTS TO NURSES AND THE SICK.

The first and most important duty of the nurse is to follow scrupulously and exactly the directions of the physician. Let no facts be concealed from him, or half told. Let no entreaties of the patient, or faith in your own experience, induce you to counteract his orders. If a person be trusted at all in this capacity, he must be trusted entirely; for health, and even life, may be sacrificed by different individuals trying experiments unknown to each other. If you think of anything which seems an improvement upon his practice, suggest it to him, and mention your reasons.

Keep the chamber well aired. Fevers are often prolonged by an unreasonable timidity about fresh air. The only precaution that is necessary is to keep your patient out of the current of it, and away from damp walls. Garments and bed-clothes should be changed more frequently in sickness than in health, and always carefully aired. If the patient is too ill to have her clothes changed every night and morning, they should be washed the oftener.

The personal cleanliness of the sick is of very great importance. The face, hands, and neck, should be washed with lukewarm soap and water every day ; do not let this be neglected from an unreasonable superstition about taking cold ; there is not the slightest danger of this, provided the patient be kept from a draught of air, and is not allowed to remain long wet. The feet should often be bathed with warm soap and water, dried with a soft cloth, and immediately covered up. Where it is possible, the hair should be combed, and the teeth brushed every day ; if weakness prevent this, let the teeth and tongue be washed with a fine linen swab.

It is an unspeakable comfort to feverish and nervous patients to have their face, hands and feet frequently sponged with warm water. It promotes moisture of the skin, and often induces a sweet sleep; even gentle rubbing with the hand is often quieting. In cases of high fever it is very refreshing to sponge the entire person with a solution made of one tea-spoonful of pearl ash, or sal-æratis, dissolved in a pint of lukewarm water—afterward wiped off with a fresh sponge dipped in warm vinegar and water. Weakly and consumptive patients are benefited by being washed in warm white rum.

Remove all impurities from the room immediately, and make free use of Chloride of Lime.

Frequently wash up the glass, crockery, and spoons that are used in a sick chamber, and do it with as little noise as possible. Keep them covered with a clean towel.

Sweep with a hand-brush and dusting-pan, to avoid dust and noise.

Let food be prepared in perfectly clean vessels, and served up to the patient in the neatest and most agreeable manner; a sticky spoon, or a greasy bowl, will often quite destroy the feeble appetite. All nourishment for the sick should often be made fresh; when warmed over, it tastes less pleasantly, and is not as apt to be wholesome. Never first taste of food yourself, or blow upon it, lest it disgust the invalid. When necessary to taste of food, to ascertain its warmth or seasoning, put away the spoon you use, without dipping it a second time.

Wash your hands frequently; and use your fingers as little as possible in preparing food or medicine.

Always carry a towel under the food or medicines you offer.

Let no importunities persuade you to indulge a patient in forbidden food; if this give great offence, inform the physician, and ascertain if any pleasant change can be safely devised. In all diseases, the safest side to err upon is keeping the diet too low and mild.

Do every thing as quietly as possible. Step lightly and gently; avoid creaking shoes, rustling garments,

2*

and banging doors; have hinges and locks oiled; lay
the coal or wood upon the fire with your hand, protected by an old glove.   A slight jarring of the bed, or
the unfolding of dry paper, sometimes makes a nervous
patient restless for the whole night.   The buzzing
sound of whispering in the room is often even more
distressing than loud talk.   A sudden stream of light
from an opened shutter, or a candle placed where the
light can be seen, is often perfect torment.

Use no snuff, or any article of food, the smell of
which may be offensive to weak nerves.   As for ardent
spirit, no person who tastes it is fit to minister to the
sick.

Ask no unnecessary questions.   Avoid the repetition
of what you perceive to be irritating.   If the mind be
wandering, appear to fall in with the train of thought,
and do not fatigue the patient by asking explanations.
Keep a cheerful countenance.   Tell no gloomy stories
about fatal accidents, especially such as occurred under
the very circumstances in which the invalid is placed
Incalculable mischief is often done by exciting the im-
agination in this way, especially during pregnancy.

Under the head of gloomy remarks, I do not mean to
include Christian conversation concerning another world.
Where it is a settled case that a human being is de-
parting, I have always thought it kind to talk openly,
and with serious cheerfulness, of the prospect before
them.   In these particulars, however, a nurse must be
guided by the wishes of relations and friends.

Preparations for the night should be made early in
the evening ; for if a drowsy patient is disturbed with
whispering, stirring the fire, passing in and out, &c., it
often breaks up sleep for the whole night.

Be very careful to get exact directions of the food
and medicine to be taken during the night : it is prudent
to make a memorandum of them.   Be scrupulous in
measuring medicines : it is best the physician should
see the size of the spoon you intend to use.   In extreme illness important results often depend upon not

varying five minutes in the prescribed time of giving medicines. It is well to keep a record of what occurs between the physician's visits, that he may accurately know the progress of the disease.

Always have a second lamp in the room, and facilities for obtaining hot and cold water.

Unless especially instructed so to do, never wake an invalid from sleep to administer nourishment. Guard their slumbers well ; for " Sleep is tired nature's sweet restorer."

In preparing medicines, remove the sticks and pods from senna ; other seed from flax-seed; dirt from roots; and all mouldy or musty parts from herbs.

When the feet are put in warm water, have the limbs well protected by blankets or flannels around the tub. Wipe one foot dry with a warm cloth, and put on a warm stocking, before the other foot is taken from the water. If the water becomes cool, add warmth to it— being careful not to scald.

When a patient is to be rubbed, it is better to make mittens of flannel or crash, because these present a more even and agreeable surface than a cloth that slips about in your hand. Do not rub backward and forward, and be careful not to injure the skin

When you make the bed, arrange the feathers so that the head and shoulders will be elevated ; and tuck in the under sheet well. Feather beds and pillows are heating when fever is present ; mattresses, or straw beds, and hair pillows, should be obtained.

Have something to throw over the patient's shoulders when sitting up. Support the back with a footstool or chair behind the pillow, and let the feet have something firm to press against. Change of posture is oftentimes an inexpressible relief.

When an invalid walks with difficulty, he may be drawn from the bed to the fire in a rocking-chair, comfortably arranged with blankets and pillows. See that the shoes are warmed in readiness ; and if pillows are brought from another room, have them well aired. A

rocking-chair gently tipped back, and securely supported by blocks, is an easy position for the weak.

When a person is too feeble to sit up long, have two
sets of pillows, sheets, and blankets, that one set may
be aired in readiness to put on.

If an invalid is removed from his own bed to one be-
side it, have the head of the second bed placed toward
the foot of the first.   The patient will thus be laid
in the same direction after moving, as before ; and
much unnecessary fatigue, and awkward lifting, will be
avoided.

If the patient cannot be moved from the bed at all,
half the sheet can be turned over in smooth folds ; a
warm clean one can be substituted, with one half of it
likewise in smooth folds ; the patient can then be moved to the clean side.

In common cases, a good nurse can judge when a
gentle emetic, or cathartic, or cooling beverage, is necessary; how much exercise is salutary ; and when a
cheerful guest may be admitted.   Loud, rapid talkers,
and excitable nervous visiters should be excluded from
the sick chamber.   That you may know what to avoid,
observe the countenance and pulse of your patient—the
temperature of the skin, and the effect of food.

Both doctors and nurses, as they grow older and
wiser, use as little medicine as possible, and simply
content themselves with recommending fasting, or such
light diet as will best assist the kindly efforts of nature.

A really good nurse must have a tender conscience,
as well as a feeling heart.   She must realize that the
slightest deviation from truth, even to screen herself
from blame, is not only a violation of the trust reposed
in her, but is a sin against God.

When her patience is severely taxed by unreasonable caprices, she must remember how sickness weakens
the mind, and try to apply the golden rule.

When infants are fretful, she must beware of the
temptation to administer opiates.   To endanger the
health, or dim the intellect of a human being, for the

sake of temporary convenience, is a fearful responsibility.

Invalids too, have Christian duties to perform. Being of necessity obliged to make a good deal of trouble, they should make as little as possible. They are bound to pay a kind regard to the comfort and convenience of those who nurse them. This may be shown by complaining as little as possible ; by a pleasant acknowledgment of affectionate attentions ; by trying to think of all they want while the nurse is up, that they may not be obliged to call her from her chair the moment she is seated ; by swallowing disagreeable medicines without an unnecessary fuss ; and by not coaxing her for food, which the doctor has forbidden.

FOOD AND DRINK FOR INVALIDS.

In almost all cases where the human frame is disordered, fasting, or very abstemious use of food, is the safest course. In cases of decided illness, the remark is strongly applicable. Dr. Dewees says,—"In almost every disease, too much anxiety is expressed for the *strength of the patient.* It does not seem to be recollected that the patient and the disease are a unit ; and when you attempt to strengthen the one, you run the risk of increasing the other ; especially if this be done with stimulating diet. Debility is not a disease—remove the disease, and you will rarely have trouble with the debility."

Fleshy, full-blooded people will do well to eat little or no animal food, especially in summer. Pickles and stimulating drinks are injurious. Porter and strong beer have a tendency to produce apoplexy in such constitutions.

Those who have humors, should avoid acids, salt provisions, nuts, butter, and all stimulating drinks. An immoderate use of honey is bad for bilious people, and those troubled with eruptions of the skin.

Those subject to restricted habits of body, should choose such articles of food as are gently laxative, viz. coarse bread, rye pudding, drinks mixed with West India molasses, &c. Many diseases might be prevented by the habitual use of such diet as promotes a healthy state of the digestive powers. People should observe what agrees with them, and regulate themselves accordingly.

People afflicted with piles should avoid stimulating food and drink, and make free use of mucilaginous articles—such as soft rye hasty-pudding, sago, slippery elm, flax-seed, &c.

Mucilaginous articles are likewise very beneficial in dysentery, diarrhea, &c. They serve to soothe internal inflammation, at the same time that they are safe nourishment. Rennet-whey is extremely salutary. Carefully abstain from meat, fermented or distilled liquors, fruits, vegetables, cakes, pies, preserves, raisins, &c. If milk is used, it should be boiled, to give it a slightly astringent quality. Milk porridge, gruel, boiled rice, with a little sugar and nutmeg ; white bread well toasted with a little perfectly sweet butter upon it, are considered the safest food. When the inflammation has entirely subsided, an egg may be taken, beat up in milk, and seasoned with loaf sugar and nutmeg ; beef tea ; chicken broth ; and finally, tender beef, or mutton broiled, and seasoned with salt and pepper. There must not be too much haste in eating these articles, as all animal food tends to increase inflammation. Use but little drink of any kind during the continuance of the disease.

Dyspeptic people should abjure pastry, cakes, and raisins, the skins of which are the most indigestible food in creation. Their bread should be made of unbolted meal, and never eaten until it has been baked a day or two. If common bread be used, it should be cut thin, and toasted very brown. If fruit be eaten, it should be perfectly ripe, and without the skin and stones.* Cranberries and currants, either in their natural state, or cooked in various forms, are deemed salutary. The gizzard of fowls, broiled and seasoned, are thought to promote digestion. Rennet whey is extremely beneficial, and should be used very freely. Different articles should not be eaten at the same meal; and it is highly advisable to taste no food between dinner and breakfast time.

Fresh pork and veal are the most indigestible of meats ; and are peculiarly unsuited to young or weak stomachs.

Where there are feverish symptoms, all preparations of animal food should be avoided ; and no wine, stimulating liquors, or spices, should be mingled with gruel, whey, or drinks of any kind. Refrigerant, quieting, and mild articles should alone be used. The signs of fever are dry, hot skin, restlessness, quick pulse, flushed face, &c.

Parsley, celery, and asparagus, have diuretic properties, and are, therefore, recommended to those who have dropsy, &c.

Those afflicted with hectic, and consumptive cough, will be comforted by a free use of honey and milk, either mixed as a drink, or eaten with other articles of food. As a laxative and expectorant, honey is much better for being boiled. Milk and West India molasses is a good substitute, as a drink. Lemonade is salutary. All such things as wines, brandy, &c. should be avoided. The general food should be simple and easy of digestion—such as arrow-root, Irish moss, blanc-mange, very ripe fruit, simple puddings, &c. Clam water and raw oysters are much recommended. Bread should be well toasted, and not used when recently baked. Eggs are sometimes recommended. If beaten up, they are more apt to disagree with the stomach than if swallowed whole. They are sometimes taken in a very

---

*Dr. Dewees says, " The common idea that it is healthy to swallow the stones of cherries, is one of the most absurd and dangerous errors that popular opinion continues to cherish." The skins of apples, peaches, &c. are very indigestive.

little port wine ; if this does not agree with the patient, they can be swallowed in milk or water. Rennet whey, or the whey left of cheese, is extremely salutary ; it promotes digestion, and is both soothing and nutritious. Butter-milk is likewise recommended. Feeble people, in the vicinity of dairies, would do wisely to make free use of these articles.

Asses' milk and goats' milk have had extensive reputation in cases of consumption ; and women's milk is said to have an efficacy superior to either. Consumptive children are reported to have been cured by sharing the breast with an infant brother or sister.

Chocolate, particularly if it be made thick, is too rich for weakly and sedentary people.

Tea is astringent and exciting. Neither that or strong coffee should be used in nervous families. Black tea is less injurious than green ; but even that, if drank at all, should be largely mixed with milk and sugar. Tea is used as medicine in nervous head-ache, and recovery from diarrhea.

Water Gruel, or Oatmeal Gruel.

Sift the meal thoroughly ; mix two table spoonfuls of it in three or four of water; when free from lumps, pour it into a pint of boiling water, and stir it frequently. Let it boil half an hour ; skim it, and season it lightly with salt ; remember it is easier to add salt than to take it out. If the patient likes it very thin, use half the quantity of meal. A handful of raisins may sometimes be boiled in it, but must not be eaten. A little white sugar and lemon-juice are sometimes added, for variety ; and where there is no fever, grated nutmeg is allowed. When milk is not forbidden, a tea-cup full boiled up once with a pint of the gruel, is an improvement.

Rye meal, or Indian, may be used ; but oatmeal is preferred, because it is more cooling, and less apt to sour upon the stomach. Rye is a good substitute, where a decidedly laxative effect is desirable.

Oatmeal gruel is bland, nutritious, and slightly laxative. Applicable to cases of fever and inflammation. Often given after brisk cathartics, to assist their operation.

Decoction of Barley, Malt Tea, &c.

Malt tea is made by pouring a quart of boiling water upon a gill and a half of ground malt. Stir it repeatedly, and let it stand till cool; then strain it. Molasses, or milk, may be added, if agreeable. Recommended to nurses, to increase milk.

Barley is the mildest and least irritating of farinaceous substances, and therefore has high reputation in cases of fever or inflammation. Pearl Barley is generally preferred, on account of its whiteness and delicacy; but common malt is as good a demulcent, and more nutritious. A simple decoction is made by boiling four ounces of malt in a quart of water, till reduced to a pint and a half, and strained. A few hops are sometimes added as a tonic, in cases of debility.

The compound decoction is made thus: one quart of the simple decoction, two ounces of sliced figs, the same of stoned raisins, half an ounce of broken and bruised liquorice root, and one pint of water. While boiling, add first the raisins, then the figs, and the liquorice just before it is finished. Boil it down to a quart, and strain it. It has the same properties as the simple decoction, and is likewise gently laxative.

Slippery Elm Gruel.

The bark is sold in fine powder. Two table-spoonfuls mixed with a very little cold water, then turned into a pint of boiling water, and cooked ten or fifteen minutes; sweetened to the taste; sometimes a sprinkle of salt. Bland and demulcent; therefore good nourishment in fevers, and particularly in dysentery and other bowel complaints.

If the powder be not at hand, the mucilaginous liquid

3

can be obtained by boiling the bark ; the thickness can easily be regulated by the addition of water.

Egg Gruel.

Boil a pint of new milk ; beat four new eggs to a light froth, and pour in while the milk boils ; stir them thoroughly together, but do not let them boil. Add a little salt, sweeten with loaf sugar, and grate in a whole nutmeg. Take half of it while warm, and the other half in two hours. Somewhat astringent, nutritious and medicinal in *advanced stages* of chronic dysentery, when the disease continues from weakness, after the cause has been removed by physic.

Wheat Mush.

Made of unbolted wheat meal boiled in water, considerably thinner than hasty-pudding is usually made. Strain it through a sieve while hot. It may be eaten in milk, or with West India molasses, several times a day. A very excellent remedy for habitual costiveness.

Hasty Pudding.

Mix five or six spoonfuls of sifted meal in half a pint of cold water ; stir it into a quart of water while boiling; season it with salt to your taste ; and from time to time sprinkle in dry meal, stirring it thoroughly. It should cook about half an hour, or three quarters. When it is so thick as to be stirred with difficulty, it is about right to suit most people. It may be eaten with milk, or molasses, or sugar. Either Indian meal, or rye, may be used ; the latter needs the least cooking, and is best adapted for a restricted state of the system, and for dyspepsia.

Milk Porridge.

Mix two table-spoonfuls of sifted flour in three or four of water ; pour it into a gill or more of boiling

water, and stir it often while it cooks, eight or ten minutes ; then add a pint of new milk, and let it boil up
once.

In cases of dysentery, it should be made thicker, and
boiled more thoroughly ; and it is well to toast the
flour quite brown before using it. Where there are no
symptoms of inflammation, salt and nutmeg may be used,
and a little loaf sugar, if the patient likes it sweet; but
in case of fever, very little salt, and no spice, should be
put into nourishment. Unless the patient is decidedly
recovering, it is best to keep to water-gruel, gum
arabic water, &c.

Chicken Broth.

Cut a chicken in quarters ; put it into three or four
quarts of water ; add a cup of rice while the water is
cold ; season it with pepper and salt. Let it stew gently until the joints fall apart. A little parsley, shred fine,
is an improvement. A few pieces of cracker may be
thrown in, if you like. This food is proper only for
quite advanced stages of convalescence. While the
stomach continues weak, it is best to separate the broth
from the rice, crackers, and other materials, and take
the liquid only.

Chicken Tea.

Separate a young, tender chicken into several pieces;
take off every particle of fat or skin ; sprinkle on a
little salt ; and let it boil half an hour. A tea spoonful
of the liquid may be given at once, and increased as
the patient can bear it. This is very salutary in cases
of cholera, and protracted diarrhea, when the weak
stomach rejects food and medicines.

Beef Tea.

Cut lean and juicy beef into inch pieces ; cork them
up closely in a wide-mouthed bottle ; keep it in boiling

water for an hour or more. In this way you get the pure juice of the meat. Season it with a little salt, and give a tea-spoonful or more, according to circumstances.

A more common way is to broil a tender steak, season it, cut it into morsels, and just cover it with water not quite boiling. Let it steep till the goodness is drawn out, then add a very little more hot water. This, like other animal nourishment, is stimulating in its nature, and is therefore unsuited to fevers, or bowel complaints accompanied with any degree of inflammation. It is proper for the weak condition that follows the removal of various diseases.

Rice.

In its common form, is picked, washed, and soaked an hour or two in water enough to cover it. Slowly boiled in the same water, until it becomes quite soft. A little salt added. Eaten with sugar ; and if the patient is well enough, nutmeg and butter may be added. For children, it is often boiled in milk instead of water. Being mucilaginous and bland, it is much used in convalescence from bowel complaints, and other diseases. It swells in cooking. A tea-cup full will make nearly a quart of pudding.

Irish Moss Blanc-Mange.

Wash the moss clean, and shake the water from each sprig. Boil about an ounce of moss in a quart of new milk, till it dissolves and attains the consistency of warm jelly. Strain it through a cloth, sweeten with powdered loaf-sugar, and season with a little rose-water, or essence of lemon. Turn it into cups or bowls, that have been wet with cold water. It will soon harden, so that it can be turned out. If you prefer cinnamon to other spices, you can easily obtain the flavor, by boiling a few sticks of it in the milk. It is very light, agreeable, and nourishing food for debilitated people.

Those who carefully observe the moss kept for sale, will be able to find plenty like it on almost any sea-beach. It requires frequent washings to clean it. When dried, it may be kept a very long time.

Slippery Elm Blanc-Mange.

Made in a manner similar to the above; the bark being boiled in new milk, till it becomes very ropy.

Calf's Foot Jelly.

Boil four feet, nicely cleaned and washed, in a gallon of water, till reduced to a quart. Strain it, and when cool scrape off the fat. In taking out the jelly, avoid the settlings. Add half a pound of sugar, the juice of four lemons, and, if you please, the peel of one. Some add the white of six eggs, to make it very clear. Boil all these together a few minutes, and strain through cloth into glasses.

In making blanc-mange, the jelly is obtained in the same way. To every quart add a quart of new milk, with sugar to your taste, and boil it ten minutes. If you wish to flavor it with sticks of cinnamon, or lemon-peel, boil them in it; if with rose-water, or peach-water, add a cupfull afterward. Strain it through a fine sieve; stir it till lukewarm; then turn it into moulds that have been wet with cold water; and let it harden. This is very strengthening food.

Starch Jelly.*

Thoroughly dissolve a table-spoonful of potato starch in a little cold water; pour it into about half a pint of

---

* Starch is thus obtained. Pare raw potatoes, grate them, place the pulp in a strainer, pass repeated portions of cold water through it into a vessel beneath. A white, farinaceous substance will be

3*

boiling water, and let it simmer a few minutes.   Stir it
well, strain it, sweeten and flavor it to your taste, and
let it cool.   Properties similar to arrow-root.

Blanc-mange may be made of this, or almost any
mucilaginous substance.

Cranberry Jelly.

Stew cranberries a little, put them in a cloth, and
squeeze out the juice.   To a quart of this add a pint of
the jelly obtained by boiling calves' feet.   Add half a
pound of white sugar, boil it up once, strain it through
cloth, and leave it to cool.

Rice Jelly.

Boil a quarter of a pound of rice-flour with half a
pound of loaf-sugar in a quart of water, till the whole
becomes a glutinous mass.   Then strain it, and let it
cool.

If you merely wish to prepare rice-water, rub a large
tea-spoonful of the flour in a table-spoonful of water,
then pour it into half a pint of boiling water, stirring
it well.   When cool, lemon-juice and sugar may be
added.

Arrow Root Jelly.

Stir a table-spoonful of arrow-root powder in half a
cup of water ; pour it into a pint of boiling water, and
let it cook six or eight minutes.   Sweeten it to your
taste.   By increasing the proportions, blanc-mange
may be made of arrow-root.   If the patient is well
enough, it may be prepared with milk, or half milk
and half water, and eaten cold with a little sugar and
cream.

When used for drink a tea-spoonful of the powder

deposited at the bottom.   Turn the water off, and let it dry thoroughly.   Frozen potatoes are said to yield more starch than others.

is moistened and rubbed with cold water ; half a pint of boiling water is turned upon it, and stirred till it becomes transparent. Lemon-juice and sugar may be added.

Tapioca Jelly—Sago Jelly.

These articles need to be picked, washed, and soaked four or five hours, before they are cooked. Boiled slowly in the same water, till it becomes entirely glutinous. A common tea-cup-full in a quart or more of water will form a thick jelly. Pearl sago is generally preferred as the most delicate preparation. Eaten cold, with sugar and cream.

Rice, arrow-root, tapioca, and sago, are all light, demulcent articles, well adapted to bowel complaints and feverish symptoms.

When the patient is *nearly recovered*, tapioca, or sago, after being duly soaked in just water enough to cover them, may be baked with the addition of milk, and two eggs well beaten. Two thirds of a cup full is enough for a quart of milk. Seasoned to taste. Baked about three quarters of an hour.

Gum Arabic Water.

Nourishing and demulcent, without any stimulating properties. It has a great tendency to allay inward inflammation. Excellent in fevers, diarrheas, and other bowel complaints. Dissolve an ounce of the gum in a pint of boiling water, and let it cool. It may be sweetened with loaf sugar. In some cases it may well form the entire food and drink of the patient. A piece of the gum held in the mouth and allowed slowly to dissolve, is very beneficial to sore throats, hard coughs, catarrhal affections, &c.

Currant Jelly.

If it be necessary to wash your currants, be sure they are thoroughly drained, or the jelly will be too

thin.   Break them up, and squeeze them through a
cloth.   A pint of clean sugar to a pint of juice ; boil it
slowly, till it becomes ropy.   Great care must be taken
not to do it too fast, lest it become scorched.   It should
be frequently skimmed and stirred while simmering.
If currants are cooked in a jar placed in boiling water,
before they are broken and strained, they are more likely to keep a long time without fermenting.   This is a
very agreeable article of food, and considered harmless
in most cases of illness, where the stomach can bear
anything of the kind.

Black Currant Jelly.

Made of black currants, in the same way.   This is
excellent for sore throats.

Preserved Barberries.

Preserved in their own weight of sugar, or molasses,
they are very useful and agreeable in sickness.   They
should simmer slowly in the sugar half an hour, or more,
until they become quite soft.   When the patient cannot
suck the fruit, the syrup is pleasant, either as food, or
stirred into drinks.   Barberries are refrigerant, anti-
scorbutic, and somewhat astringent.

Stewed Peaches.

Peaches pared and stewed with sugar, form an excellent laxative article of diet in convalescence from bowel
complaints.

Stewed Prunes.

Stew them very gently in a small quantity of water,
till the stones slip out.   They are slightly laxative and
cooling.   Considered safe nourishment in fevers.
Taken too largely, when the stomach is debilitated,
they occasion flatulence.   The water in which they

are cooked is pleasant to moisten the parched lips of
an invalid.

Figs.

Nutritious, laxative, and demulcent. If eaten too
freely, sometimes produce diarrhea. All dried fruits,
excepting figs and prunes, are difficult of digestion.

Quince Syrup.

The syrup of preserved quinces is a good addition to
drinks in cases of dysentery, after inflammation has subsided. Astringent properties.

Conserve of Roses.

Bruise the red leaves of roses in a wooden or
marble mortar.   To every pound, allow a pound
of sugar.   Mix the sugar well with the roses, in
alternate layers, pack it tight in an earthen vessel,
and cover it very carefully from the air.   It will
keep a great while.   Pleasant, slightly astringent, and
considered very strengthening to weakly people.

Wild Honeysuckle Conserve.

The Wild Honeysuckle, or Swamp Pink, is common among brushwood in low land.   Botanists have
named it *Azalea Viscosa*.   The blossoms closely
resemble the cultivated honey suckle.   They are
hairy, and very glutinous.   A conserve made of
them, in the same way as roses, is considered
very strengthening, and is much used by consumptive
people.

Sorrel Conserve.

Common field Sorrel, or *Rumex Acetosella*, is
well known as a troublesome weed.   Wood Sorrel, or
Oxalis Acetosella, has light green heart-shaped leaves,

three together on a slender stem. Small flowers, generally yellow. Sorrel is acid, refrigerant, and diuretic. Used as salad, or boiled as greens, recommended in scorbutic complaints. A conserve of the fresh leaves, with double their weight of sugar, is a good substitute for lemons. Used in inflammatory disorders.

Violet Syrup.

The sweet English Violet, or the wild Purple Violet, or the large Blue Violet, may be used. The two first are preferred. Pour three pints of boiling water upon a pound of the fresh flowers, and let them steep twenty-four hours in an *earthen* vessel. Strain through linen without squeezing. To every pint of the liquid add twenty-nine ounces of sugar, and boil it up a few minutes. This syrup has a very beautiful color, gradually lost by age. It is much recommended as a mild laxative for children. Infants may take a table-spoonful, or half that quantity, according to age.

Syrup of White Poppies.

Two pounds of the seed-vessels, freed from seed, may be sliced and boiled about an hour in fifteen quarts of water ; strain them by squeezing strongly, and boil it down one half. Lastly, add four pounds of sugar, and let it simmer a few minutes. This syrup is an opiate of uncertain strength, and should be used sparingly till tested by experience. A tea-spoonful may be given to an infant of six months, and a dessert-spoonful to one of two years. This may be repeated every three or four hours, if necessary.

Yellow Water-Lily Syrup.

In Bigelow's Botany, the plant is called *Nuphar Advena.* The mucilaginous roots, cut in slices and baked with sugar, form a syrup resembling honey. It promotes expectoration, and is mild and nourishing for consumptive people.

Wine Whey.

Place half a pint of sweet milk at the fire in an earthen or silver vessel. When near the boiling point, pour in one glass of wine, and let it remain perfectly still in a cool place till it curdles. When the curds settle, strain the whey, and let it cool. A spoonful of rennet-water hastens the process. Made palatable with loaf sugar; and sometimes nutmeg, if the patient can bear it. Wine whey is not powerful as a stimulant; but it is sufficiently so not to be used when fevers run high, or when there is any inflammation of the bowels. It is applicable after fevers have turned, and to the weak condition that follows diarrhea. Pure Madeira, or Sherry, are the best kinds of wine to use.

Orange Whey.

The juice of a large acid orange to a quart of warm milk. If the curds do not separate easily, boil it a little, and strain the liquor. Sweeten to the taste.

Lemon Whey.

Prepared in the same way. This whey is used in high fevers, on account of its cooling qualities.

Vinegar Whey.

To warm milk add as much vinegar as will produce curds; probably about a wine-glass to a pint; but it would vary with the strength of the vinegar, which should be made of cider.

This is less heating than wine whey, and promotes perspiration equally well. Sometimes advisable to dilute it with water.

Cider Whey.

Prepared in the same manner, and similar in its qualities. Cider, being less strong than vinegar, would be required in larger quantities.   Some people boil it a little, if the curds do not separate well.

In making any kind of whey, or curds, the liquid should remain quite undisturbed during the process.

Sorrel Whey.

Made by boiling Sorrel leaves in new milk.   Cooling in fevers.

Molasses Whey.

Heat a quart of new milk nearly to the boiling point; stir in a wine-glass of molasses ; when cool, strain off the whey to drink.   Good for nurses, who have an insufficiency of milk.

Rennet Whey.

Soak a piece of well-cured rennet, about an inch square, in little more than half a tea-cup-full of water, over night.   Put both the rennet and the water into a pint of new milk, about blood-warm, and let it stand quietly in the chimney corner, till the curds separate ; then strain it.   A little sweetening may be added, if you like it.   This is recommended to dyspeptic people, because it is light nourishment, and assists digestion.   Very salutary for weakly, consumptive people. Dr. Dewees says it answers an admirable purpose, both as nourishment and drink, in cases of bilious diarrhea, often called " the summer complaint."

Said to be good for the heart-burn.

Mustard Whey.

Boil half an ounce of the powdered seed in a pint of new milk; strain it, and sweeten with sugar.   A wine-glass-full may be drank several times a day.   Given in cases of low, nervous fever.   It greatly warms and invigorates the system, and promotes the different secretions.   Sometimes it is well to dilute the whey with a little water.

Milk of Almonds.

The kind used are sold under the name of sweet
almonds. Shell them, and pour over them hot water,
not quite boiling. Let them remain a few minutes, and
the brown shell will be easily peeled off. This is called blanching. Put a tea-cup-full into a wooden or
marble mortar, with half a cup-full of warm water;
grind them slowly with the pestle; increase the water
from time to time till you have put in half a pint; still
continuing to grind, till the goodness appears to be
thoroughly extracted. Then stir the liquid well, and
strain it through muslin. It should be made fresh often,
as it sours if kept more than one day in warm weather.

This milky substance is of a pleasant flavor. A little loaf sugar may be added, if the patient likes it. Demulcent, and slightly astringent. Light, nutritious food
in cases of consumption, dysentery, and bowel-com-
plaints. Recommended in catarrh, and to obviate
stranguary during the application of a blister. Used
externally as a cosmetic.

Apple Water.

Apples may be roasted, boiling water poured over
them, and steeped two or three hours; or the boiling
water may be poured on sour apples, pared and sliced,
strewed with sugar, and bits of lemon-peel; or three
common-sized tart apples may be boiled in a quart of
water, till reduced to pulp. Strained and sweetened.
Used as light nourishment, when the stomach is too
weak to bear more common preparations. Dried apples may be used, if more convenient.

Lemonade.

Pour a pint of boiling water upon a table-spoonful of
lemon juice, sweeten it to your taste, and place it where
it will become cool. Some like to have a few pieces
of the peel remain to season it. A very pleasant

4

drink can be made by simply adding cold water and sugar to the juice. A very agreeable and cooling beverage in fevers.

Currant Water.

The juice of currants, obtained by squeezing through a cloth, mixed with water and sugar, is a very good substitute for lemonade.

Barberry Water.

The same may be said of barberries, macerated in water, strained, and sweetened.

Tamarind Water.

Half a pint of boiling water poured upon two or three table-spoonfuls of preserved Tamarinds ; after standing a little while, strained and cooled ; forms a pleasant beverage in fevers. Refrigerant and somewhat laxative.

Sorrel Water.

Made by steeping the bruised leaves in water, till they yield their acid.

Cream of Tartar.

Place one or two tea-spoonfuls of cream of tartar and the rind of one lemon in an earthen vessel ; pour over them a quart of boiling water. When cold, sweeten it to your taste. Often used in fevers.

Flax Seed Tea.

Pour a quart of boiling water upon a cup-full of the seed ; let it steep ten or fifteen minutes, then turn off the water, and pour on a fresh supply. Let it steep till it becomes somewhat ropy. A tumbler full may be taken at a time ; sweetened with honey, molasses, or sugar. It is a mucilaginous demulcent fluid, very salutary for hard coughs, catarrh, dysentery, piles, stranguary, calculous affections, and other inflammatory states of the lungs and passages.

For severe colds attended with feverish symptoms, the following is an excellent remedy. Hot flax-seed tea, with lemon-juice and sugar, and fifteen drops of wine of ipecac taken when getting into a warm bed. The ipecac produces perspiration, and care should be taken about being exposed to the air the next day. If obliged to go abroad, the same preparation can be taken cold; a few spoonfuls whenever there is inclination to cough. Some add two or three spoonfuls of white-mixture, or one tea-spoonful of paregoric to a tumbler full.

Bran Water.

Wheat bran boiled in water and strained, forms a healing drink, when the bowels are disordered. Rye-bran is more laxative than wheat. It may be sweetened with molasses, if the patient chooses. Recommended as a morning drink to those troubled with restricted habits.

Toast and Water.

West India molasses and water, with a little lemon juice, and a piece of toasted bread soaked in it, is a nutritious and grateful beverage in fevers.

Sugar and Water.

When the stomach is so very feeble as to reject all kinds of nourishment, strength may be preserved for some time, by now and then giving a tea-spoonful of loaf sugar and water, well dissolved and mixed.

Dyspepsia Bread.

Three quarts of unbolted wheat meal; one quart of soft, warm water, not hot; a gill of fresh yeast; a gill of molasses, or not, as may suit the taste ; one tea-spoonful of sal-æratis. This will make two loaves, and should remain in the oven at least an hour. It will need from eight to twelve hours to rise in readiness for baking. The fermentation is, of course, more rapid when the weather is warm.

Dyspepsia crackers are made with unbolted flour, water, and sal-æratis.

It is unhealthy for any person to eat warm bread, and peculiarly so for those troubled with dyspepsia.

Bread made with the bran in it, is far more healthy for the digestive powers than flour bread.

Custards.

These should not be eaten, except in an advanced stage of convalescence. If boiled, they are lighter than baked. Of the latter, an invalid may sometimes take a few spoonfuls of the *whey*.

Four eggs are enough to allow to a quart of new milk. Boil the milk with a stick of cinnamon, or few bits of lemon-peel ; while boiling, turn it to the eggs, previously well beaten. Stir it well all the time. Sweeten it to your taste. Place the custard in a pan of boiling water, and let it simmer till it thickens, but do not let it boil. Stir it one way all the time. The custard should be in a vessel deep enough to prevent the water in the pan from boiling over the edges.

CHILDREN.

If a mother indulge violent temper, or habitual gloom and discontent, before the birth of her child, it is very apt to have an unfavorable effect both on the character and health of the infant. She should try to keep as equable as possible, and, as far as circumstances will permit, indulge in cheerful conversation and the sight of pleasant things. It is a duty to make considerable effort to resist melancholy and fretfulness.

Articles of food that disagree with the system should be scrupulously avoided. It is of great importance that the digestive powers be kept in good order. Laxative diet is the best, unless the state of the system render it improper. The common notion that more food is required during pregnancy, is false and injurious. An overcharged stomach is always unfavorable to safe and healthy labor. For this reason nature institutes nausea and vomiting, to prevent too great fulness. There is more danger from eating too much, than not enough.

Avoid using ardent spirit, tinctures, and essences, to overcome nausea. Confirmed habits of intemperance are often thus formed, and transmitted to the child. It is far better to resort to charcoal for this purpose.

Exercise in the open air is very beneficial during the first months ; but the latter part of the time it is best to avoid great fatigue.

Those subject to miscarriage should not try blood-letting without advice; it sometimes produces the evil it is intended to remedy.

During recovery from confinement, the room should not be too hot, and the fresh air should be freely admitted, provided the patient is not in the current of it. Curtains are bad things ; if circumstances render anything of the kind necessary, it is better to make use of a temporary screen. Change linen and bed-clothes often ; being careful that they are well aired.

Avoid seeing too much company, or too soon. It is better not to see even intimate friends under a week or ten days.

Take a little moderate exercise in the open air, as soon as you have strength ; for this purpose choose the forenoon of a dry, mild day. Be very careful about exposure to cold, or sitting with the feet on cold, painted floors.

Much mischief is done by too early use of stimulat-

4*

ing food and drink. Broth, wine, spices, &c. have a tendency to bring on " milk fever." The diet should consist entirely of very bland and simple articles, at least till the sixth day.

The infant should be allowed to nurse as soon as strength permits ; probably in twelve or twenty-four hours ; and it should be repeated every three or four hours. Before the birth of the child, there is an accumulation of a dark green substance in its bowels, called *meconium* ; the very first substance that comes into the mother's breast is nature's remedy for this ; and usually there is no manner of need of any other purgatives. But if the child be not applied to the breast early enough, or from any other cause the *meconium* remain, some very mild and gentle physic should be given ; such as a little warm molasses and water, or manna in water ; or a tea-spoonful of warm sweet oil ; or, in very obstinate cases, a tea-spoonful of warm castor oil. When the discharges become yellow, the repetition of such medicines is unnecessary.

Infants generally need no medicines. The hurtful practice of drugging them cannot be too much blamed.

A newly-born infant should be rubbed with fresh lard, and then carefully washed with luke-warm water, and fine old soap. A very soft flannel, or sponge, is better than linen or cotton. Care should be taken to cleanse every fold of the skin, under the arm-pits, &c. The use of cold water often produces cholic, catarrhal affections, &c. Children should not remain wet longer than is necessary, particularly in winter. Dry and warm clothes should be put on as soon as possible. The head should be first washed and wiped dry, before other parts of the body are wet. The use of brandy or rum for this purpose is unnecessary and improper. The process should not be performed in a current of air, neither should children be roused from sleep for the purpose. Every part and portion of the body ought to be thoroughly washed every morning.

If the breasts of new-born children are swollen and

inflamed, tney should not be pressed in compliance with the common but very erroneous idea that there is milk which needs to be extracted ; serious injury to the part is sometimes done in this way. A piece of old linen moistened with pure sweet oil, or fresh lard, is usually all that is necessary ; and if the inflammation be uncommon, a bread and milk poultice, every three or four hours, will be quite sufficient.

The use of fine delicate soap and water is at once a preventative and remedy for the chafing of the skin so common behind the ears, under the arm-pits, &c. It should be wiped quite dry with a soft rag. Starch, powdered and sifted through muslin, may be applied when there is extensive chafing. Flour, toasted brown, likewise answers a good purpose. When moisture appears, an additional quantity should be put on, without removing the first until the child is washed. In a little time it will fall off spontaneously.

The mother's milk is the only proper nourishment. Nothing but the most imperious necessity should induce a departure from this obvious rule of nature. The healthiest children are those who for six months at least were never fed with any other substance.

The mother should scrupulously refrain from all such articles as disagree with her. Unripe fruit, cabbage, pickles, vinegar, porter and beer, almost always hurt the child, because they are injurious to the mother. It is important the digestive powers be kept in good order, by the judicious use of laxative diet, when circumstances require it.

Avoid all over-heating, from running, dancing, excessive fatigue, &c. ; likewise the indulgence of violent passions, or emotions. If anything of this kind takes place, do not nurse the child for at least two hours after the occurrence, lest convulsion-fits should be the consequence.

A child constantly nursed from one breast is apt to grow crooked, and acquire the habit of squinting, from having the eyes constantly directed to one point. There are similar objections to its being carried always on one arm, or laid on one side.

It is a good habit to nurse an infant the last thing before going to bed. Avoid letting it go to sleep at the breast. This habit weakens the mother, and is apt to injure the digestive powers of the child.

It is a bad plan to nurse a child whenever it cries; and still worse to feed it with pap. By this means it forms the habit of requiring more nourishment than its stomach can well bear.

For those afflicted with sore nipples, the following preparation is healing and pleasant. Put twenty grains of sugar-of-lead into one gill of rose-water; shake it thoroughly. Wet a piece of soft linen with it, and put it on; renew it as often as the rag becomes dry. Before nursing, wash this off with something soothing. Rose-water will answer; but the best thing is a glutinous solution made by steeping quince-seed in a little cold tea.

The author of the Maternal Physician states a curious fact. He says when the process of nursing is very painful to the mother, the milk is sometimes drawn out with sucking-glasses; if the child is fed with it, a supply will remain in the breast some time; whereas, if it is thrown away, it will gradually diminish till it ceases.

Hard, tight corsets are very hurtful at any time; and peculiarly so to pregnant and nursing women.

A failure or deficiency of milk more often proceeds from an over than an under quantity of food or drink. There should be enough of simple and nutritious diet; but such stimulating articles as milk-punch and porter should be avoided. The best things for improvement of milk are exercise in the open air, and the free use of milk, malt tea, and molasses whey.

If a mother have not milk enough to nourish her child, the best substitute consists of two-thirds *new* milk, one third water, and a little loaf sugar; made fresh often, and given luke-warm. Some prefer perfectly sweet cream to milk, because they consider it lighter. After several teeth have been cut, a little rice water, or gum-arabic water may be added to the preparation. When from bowel complaints, or other causes, it is desirable to diminish the *quantity* of food, it is well to increase its nutritious qualities in this way—particularly by the addition of gum arabic.

Potatoes and other vegetables are very bad for infants; especially if they be mashed with gravy. Such unnatural kind of food lays the foundation for many humors and diseases.

Babes are generally weaned in about a year. Nature seems to indicate the propriety of this; for after the twelfth or fourteenth month, the milk deteriorates in quality and quantity. April, May, and June are considered suitable months for weaning, because the temperature is then moderate. In hot weather there is great danger of inducing bowel complaints. October is the best time in autumn; though early in November will answer. After that, the nights are too long, and the weather too cold. If children are any way disordered, it is best to nurse them until they recover, as the change is apt to increase their illness.

The process of weaning might be rendered more easy, if for some time previous the child were accustomed to do without food in the night; if the breast were gradually given at longer intervals; and bread and milk, rice and milk, or arrow-root, substituted as nourishment.

When you have laid down a rule, an occasional departure from it only occasions additional trouble for yourself and child; a gentle firmness is the truest kindness. Sometimes it becomes necessary to render the fountain of their infant pleasure disagreeable to them, by putting on garlic, assafœtida, &c.

Great care must be taken, after weaning, not to give a child too much, or too gross food. New milk and stale bread are wholesome. An ounce of gum arabic dissolved in a pint of water, with sugar and a little milk added, is more apt to agree with the stomach than any other substance. Rennet-whey, a little sweetened and disguised with milk, is excellent.

The weaning mother, who wishes to avoid swollen and painful breasts, should drink nothing but pure water, and that in small quantities. In order to avoid the disposition to drink, it is better not to use salt provisions. Her food should consist of crackers, boiled rice with sugar and nutmeg, potatoes, poultry, &c.

If the pain be considerable, let her take a brisk dose of salts, and avoid exercise as much as she conveniently can. If the breasts be hard and swollen, dip old linen in perfectly *sweet* mutton tallow melted, and spread it over the breasts, and under the arm. If tallow cannot be obtained, use *fresh* lard, or *pure* sweet oil. It is best to have the milk drawn as seldom as can be endured, and in as small quantities, the intervals of drawing being each time longer.

Where there is an absolute necessity for feeding infants much by hand, the tea-spoon, or bottles with silver tubes, are not considered as good as the oblong flat bottle, with sponge covered with a heifer's teat, prepared by some person who understands it. This kind of bottle can be put into the bed and kept warm during the night by the heat of the body. What remains after feeding the child should be turned out, the bottle and sponge thoroughly cleansed with scalding water, and rinsed before it is again used; it should be tied with clean thread each time. Great care should be taken that everything used in feeding infants should be perfectly fresh and sweet.

Babes ought not to have the bottle to play with. They acquire the habit of sucking it every few minutes, which is injurious to their digestive powers. As a general rule, they do not need to be fed oftener than every three or four hours. Never offer more than they seem to desire. Experience alone can decide the quantities that will agree with different individuals.

Milk should not be boiled for infants. It is best new from the cow. Mere scalding will preserve it sweet, in warm weather.

Jolting, and other violent motions, are very bad for children soon after they have been fed.

They should not be fed lying down ; nor should they be laid on the back to sleep, lest suffocation from their rising food be the consequence.

When babes are very weakly, it is considered more safe to hire a wet nurse than to bring them up by hand. This step is involved with many difficulties. If the nurse have her own child with her, she is naturally tempted to give it a greater proportion of nourishment ; if the child be removed, there is the painful consideration of deriving benefit from the privations and sacrifices of another ; however conscientious she may be, it is more difficult to perform her duties patiently and well for mere money, than it is from instinct, or feeling ; hence the great danger of injuring a babe by putting it to sleep with laudanum.

If, unfortunately, there is an absolute necessity of delegating to a stranger the sacred office of a nurse, be careful that she is a healthy woman ; under thirty-five years of age ; free from humors ; from intemperate, or gluttonous habits; and not violent in her temper. Her milk should be as near the age of her nursling as possible ; it had better be younger than older. She should make very little change in her diet and mode of life. If she has been accustomed to active exercise, let it be continued ; if her food has been simple, it will injure her milk to resort to rich living.

The belly-band of an infant should be worn at least four months. It is commonly supposed that the tighter this bandage is drawn the better. This is a mistake ; too tight drawing may produce the very rupture it is intended to remedy. It should always be made of soft flannel, cut cross-wise, so as to be elastic. A little piece sewed upon it to fasten it to the diaper is convenient. A scorched linen rag, with *fresh* mutton tallow on it, or a raisin split open, are suitable to apply when the cord drops off, five or six days after birth. If there is any swelling, or unusual appearance about the navel, make it known to the doctor immediately.

Children should not remain wet. Some people talk of hardening them by neglect ; but it only exposes them to rickets, colds, inflammations, &c. They ought to be kept comfortably warm and dry at all times.

Their clothing, particularly diapers, should be washed often enough to be kept perfectly soft and sweet.

As far as possible, use strings instead of pins. The use of needles is extremely dangerous. They easily slip into the tender flesh, and produce very painful swellings. If a needle is broken or lost on the floor, there should be diligent care to find it, and put it out of the way ; particularly if there be a carpet in the room.

Cradles should never be rocked violently, lest it produce dropsy on the brain.

Children of tender age should not be carried from a warm room into a cold one. They are less liable to take cold if not accustomed to very warm rooms.

Infants should always be carried in such a manner as to support the back and the neck. Many diseases of the spine originate in a want of this precaution. The habit of tying them into chairs too young, or allowing them to remain too long, is extremely injurious, and sometimes fatal; deformed backs, ruptured bowels, and perpetual feebleness, may be the result. They had far better be laid upon a piece of carpet on the floor, and suffered to roll about and use their limbs in freedom.

Their clothes should be of soft materials, every part perfectly loose and easy, and not pinned up, so as to obstruct the motion of their feet and limbs. Warm socks and large soft shoes should be put on in cold weather.

Exercise in the open air is extremely healthy. Don't be afraid to let children be out in dry weather, and play in the dirt as much as they will; provided they are daily washed thoroughly, and have clean inner clothes at least twice a week, to prevent diseases of the skin.

Baby-carriages should have a wide axle, and low wheels, well secured against coming off, in order to guard against accidents from turning over. Its length should admit of lying down, and its depth prevent the danger of falling out. The child should be placed with its back well supported, its head elevated, and eyes carefully screened from the sun. It should not be jerked, or put into violent motion, but drawn equally and gently ; and never left standing in the sunshine, or the cold air. Half an hour at a time is exercise enough. They should be brought home when drowsy ; because it is injurious to sleep in the open air, and they will soon form the habit of going to sleep in no other way.

Children should not be urged to walk too soon, lest crooked limbs be the consequence. Let them creep if they choose, and try their own experiments of "finding their feet," by the aid of a chair, &c. In this, and many other things, it is best to let nature do her own work, with no more interference than is absolutely necessary.

The head should not be too warmly covered. Physicians almost universally recommend that infants should go without caps, and little boys and girls wear light hats and bonnets. It is better to keep the hair cut, than to have it attain a thick growth at an early age.

Keeping the throat properly protected, when out doors diminishes the liability to take cold, croup, &c.

When children get their stockings and garments wet from being exposed to rain, or heavy dews, they should be immediately changed for dry ones. There is a common idea that it hardens children to remain wet and cold ; but many die in the hardening. The feet particularly should be kept dry and warm.

Early to bed and early to rise, is a peculiarly valuable maxim applied to children. When small they should go to bed at dark, and at eight or nine o'clock when older. Their natural disposition to be stirring early in the

5

morning ought not to be checked, though it be inconvenient. Let them sleep on mattrasses, or straw, unless the weather is very cold. Give them breakfast before they have been long up.

Too much cannot be said in praise of frequently and thoroughly washing every part of the body; provided it be not performed in a current of air, and while the blood is heated with exercise. A child of a year old may be daily washed in water less than luke-warm. At all ages it is best to have the chill off; for a very cold bath disagrees with many constitutions, and sometimes does serious injury. The teeth should be washed, and the mouth rinsed ; and the hair washed in cool water, and well brushed.

Those are the healthiest children who eat the least animal food. A variety of vegetables at the same meal is decidedly injurious.

Fruit is not good for children under two years old ; as is often shown by its passing through them unchanged. After that time, reasonable quantities are not injurious, provided it be perfectly ripe. Dried fruit is more or less hurtful. Raisins sometimes produce convulsions. Large quantities of orange-peel have the same effect.

If young children are allowed to eat pies, the cooked fruit should be given them without the pastry.

Pure water, or molasses and water, is the only suitable drink for children. Much of moral, as well as bodily health, depends on the strict observance of this rule.

Half the disorders of children might be prevented by observing the state of their digestive organs, and regulating diet accordingly. The frequent use of medicines is a bad habit.

Let their clothes be large enough for perfect ease. Avoid all manner of stays, belts, or braces ; these things impede the free action of the lungs and heart, and prevent the chest from acquiring healthy dimensions.

Shoes ought to be quite large enough, and well fitted to the foot. The step is more free when stockings are habitually fastened above the knee, and never too tightly.

Children who always sleep on one side of the bed, or sit in one position at a writing-desk, or table, are apt to grow one-sided.

Those inclined to stoop forward should often march with a moderate weight balanced on the head.

Tickling, and pressing fingers on the eyes in sport, are practices attended with danger. Lifting children by the head, so that the whole weight hangs on the neck, has sometimes occasioned *instant death*.

Girls of twelve years old should be candidly told of an approaching change in their constitution, which makes it very hazardous for them to wet their feet, or stand in damp, cold places; particularly after they have been exercising. Thousands of victims are sacrificed to the false delicacy of mothers.

CHILDREN'S MEDICINES.

Table to assist the judgment with regard to doses.

If a child of 12 years, take -	8 grains.
From 8 to 10 years - - -	6 ⅔ do.
From 5 to 7 years - -	6 do.
From 3 to 4 years - - -	5 do.
Of 2 years - - • -	4 do.
From 1 year to 18 months - -	3 do.
From 9 months to 1 year -	2 ⅔ do.
From 5 months to 8 months -	2 do.
From 2 months to 4 months -	1 do.
Of 1 month - - - -	½ do.

Medicines must not only be varied according to age, but according to the constitutions of a child, and experience of their effects. One constitution will be strongly operated upon by a dose that scarcely influences another. A change of diet will often prevent the need of medicine; and where it will answer the purpose, it is always decidedly preferable.

Do not administer remedies in ardent spirits; particularly if they be at all agreeable. An early fondness for liquor is sometimes thus acquired.

Castor Oil

Is one of the best cathartics for children. Castor oil should be made thin by warming before it is given; and is easiest to take when not mixed with anything else. A large tea-spoonful is a dose for a child from one month to three months old; a dessert-spoonful for one from three to nine months old; a table-spoonful for one from nine months to two years old. These are, of course, mere general directions. Increasing, diminishing, or repeating the dose must be regulated by circumstances, of which the nurse must judge. This medicine may be increased more safely than any other.

When children have an insuperable objection to taking Castor oil, it may be effectually disguised in the following manner. Boil it with an equal quantity of new milk, sweeten it with sugar, and when cold give it to them for drink. They will often love the taste of it.

Magnesia.

Considered one of the most proper medicines for young children. Adapted to an acid state of the stomach. One tea-spoonful may be given to a child of two months; a large tea-spoonful to a child of two years. Best given thoroughly mixed with a little sweetened milk.

Senna and Jalap.

Four grains of each, mixed with eight grains of sugar, is a cathartic powder for a child of two years.

Rhubarb and Senna.

Rhubarb, six grains ; senna powder, five grains ; mixed, and taken in syrup, or molasses. A mild cathartic for a child of two years.

Flake Manna.

This is generally given as sweetening in the food or drink of children. About quarter of an ounce for an infant of two months ; half an ounce for a child of two years.

Rhubarb Tea.

Pour a wine-glass of boiling water on half a drachm of bruised rhubarb. When it is cool, strain it and sweeten it. To a child of two years a tea-spoonful may be given every two hours, until the color of the discharges are changed by it.

Ipecacuanha Wine.

One tea-spoonful is usually an emetic for a child of two years; and the same effect will be produced by five grains of the powder. There is no risk in repeating doses of Ipecac.

Laudanum.

Half a drop for a child under ten days old ; this may be measured by putting a whole drop in some liquid, and then giving half the quantity. An infant of a month old, may take one drop; from that time to three months, a drop and a half; from that age to nine months, three drops; from nine months to eighteen, four drops ; from that time to three years, five or six drops ; for each succeeding year, a drop or two may be added. These rules are founded upon the supposition that the child is unaccustomed to its use. As an injection the quantity

5*

for each age may be safely increased three or four fold. Its qualities quieting, and very astringent. When laudanum is old, it becomes thick, and is then much more powerful; in such a state, children have been killed by doses that would not otherwise have injured them.

Paregoric, which is a weaker form of opium, is given to children, from five to twenty drops, according to the age.

The free use of opiates cannot be too severely blamed. Selfish nurses and careless mothers are too apt to resort to them for the sake of putting a fretful child to sleep; and if they do not kill the poor creature, their consciences are undisturbed. Fatal accidents are probably rare; but the rickets, and other diseases, are often the consequences of this bad habit; and thousands of children have their intellects stupified by it. It should not be given except when distress renders it absolutely necessary. Children, or young people, should never be allowed to administer it to infants; neither should they be trusted to measure it for themselves—not even a few drops to apply to an aching tooth.

DISEASES OF CHILDREN.

Red Gum.

THIS consists of a small number of red pimples covering the body, generally in the course of a month after its birth. When it does not appear, there is often an injudicious desire to invite its appearance, by keeping the babe unusually warm, and feeding with stimulating teas, such as sweet marjoram, saffron, catnip, &c. It is far better to leave nature to its course. Children who are kept in a moderate temperature, who depend entirely upon the breast, and have been purged of the *meconium*, seldom have this disease.

If it does appear, it is merely necessary to wash it daily in warm water ; avoid the cold bath, and currents of air; and if the child be costive, administer some very gentle laxative. If struck in by external cold, it sometimes occasions alarming symptoms, such as difficulty of breathing, spasmodic twitchings, cold skin, &c. In this case the child should remain in a warm bath until its skin acquire warmth ; it should then be well dried, and wrapped in warm flannel. At the same time some mild stimulant, such as sweet marjoram tea, should be given. The same observations apply to the White Gum, which consists of numerous hard, whitish specks.

Scurf.

A crust that early forms on the top of the head. It is generally owing to neglect, arising from the idea that it is wrong to remove it ; but, without timely care, it may produce ulceration, and the disease called Scald Head. To prevent it, all that is necessary is to wash the head every morning with luke-warm water and fine soap, wipe it with soft flannel, and brush it gently. The use of a fine ivory comb generally produces irritation and increases the scurf. After the incrustation is formed, it should be rubbed at night with *sweet* oil or *fresh* lard, and washed off in the morning with a strong solution of borax and water, applied a little warm, and repeated daily until the scurf is removed. The solution is made by dissolving an ounce of borax in three half pints of boiling water.

Scald Head.

Ulcers form among the roots of the hair, discharge offensive matter, and gradually spread. The disease is infectious, and difficult to be cured. It originates in want of cleanliness. The head should be kept closely shaven, and daily washed with soap-suds, or lime-water. Thorn-apple ointment, rubbed on gently every night, is said to be the best remedy. Ointment made of tar and sulphur is likewise recommended. The diet should be very simple, and the bowels kept open by mild laxaatives, such as senna, jalap and senna in powder, &c. The danger of taking cold ought to be avoided. The infectious ring-worm, so called on account of very small bladder-like pimples, extending in circles, generally appears on the head and eye-brows. It should be treated in the same manner as Scald Head. The Spirits of Hartshorn, applied several times a day, has proved a cure. Physic should be taken at the same time.

Crusta Lactea.

This usually begins on the cheeks or forehead of nursing children, and gradually spreads. It consists of small whitish bunches upon a very red surface ; they change to yellow or brown, and break. It is troublesome, on account of itching day and night ; but rarely does any mischief, and leaves no scar.

In order to have it pass lightly, all stimulating articles should be avoided. If the child be at the breast, it should be nursed less frequently, and the mother strictly confined to a milk and vegetable diet ; if weaned, less milk should be given, and its food consist principally of thin arrow-root, or rennet-whey. At the same time small doses of sulphur, or sulphur and magnesia may be given, to keep the bowels gently open, but not purged.

This disease sometimes assumes a violent form, and it becomes necessary to use tar ointment, and a decoction of Lady's Delights. When the discharge is acrid, it is well to wash the surrounding parts with fine soap and water several times a day, and then rub on a little fresh lard and bees-wax melted together, to prevent its spreading.

Humors.

Little children are often troubled with eruptions from heat, which render them uncomfortable and fretful. It is a great comfort to them to be sponged several times a day with luke-warm milk and water.

Rye-flour allays the tingling of humors, and absorbs the irritating secretions; wheat-flour is often used, but is less serviceable. Powdered starch is sprinkled on the skin for the same purpose.

The late Dr. Danforth very highly recommended the use of soap in all common cutaneous eruptions. It promotes frequent cleansing of the surface, which is of the utmost importance; and it destroys the irritating secretions. Moisten hard soap, and rub it plentifully on the humor, with the fingers, or a soft rag. It should be renewed once or twice a day. When a burning, itching sensation makes children restless in the night, this application often gives relief; and there is no danger of striking the humors inward. The older soap is, the better for all medicinal purposes. The finer kinds, such as Castile and old Windsor, are most apprpriate for infants, because their skin is so tender.

The most inveterate humors have been cured by the persevering use of dock-root ointment, and drinking a decoction of the root at the same time. Whenever this and similar external applications are made, it is well to take occasionally a tea-spoonful of flour of sulphur, stirred in molasses, and as often as once a week a moderate dose of salts. The diet should be light, and no acid or stimulating articles used.

In case of sudden and violent eruptions, it is always prudent to consult a physician concerning their nature.

The attempt to scatter humors with sugar of lead, and similar applications, is hazardous, and sometimes fatal; especially if saline purgatives be not taken at the same time, and strong snake-root, to defend the stomach. Of the soothing ointment, houseleek and plantain freshly made, is one of the best.

Water from a blacksmith's forge, or any water in which hot iron has been repeatedly cooled, is excellent to bathe scrofulous and other humors.

Sore Ears.

Chafing behind the ears may be healed by frequent washing with warm milk and water, or fine soap and water ; but from a false idea that they form a necessary drain for the body, they are often permitted to become ulcerated sores, at once painful and offensive. In this case, the child, if weaned, ought to live entirely upon such articles as rice, arrow-root, and sago. The sores should be frequently bathed with milk and water, or fine soap and luke-warm water. Gentle purgatives are to be administered. Avoid laying the child to sleep upon the side affected, because warmth is injurious : for the same reason, no cap should be worn. If the child is disposed to scratch, let the hands be muffled. Bees-wax and fresh lard form a soothing salve. In case of great irritation a soft bread and milk poultice, confined in a bag of fine old linen, and applied every four or five hours, is useful ; it should be taken off as soon as the inflammation is subdued, lest it draw humors around the margin.

Babys' Sore Mouths.

This generally begins at the corners of the mouth, in little eruptions resembling a coagulum of milk, and soon spreads over the tongue and gums. In its milder forms it is very white, but when more severe is dark brown, or very red. The child slavers very much, and is evidently pained in sucking. There is generally a great inclination to sleep, though the nap is often disturbed by irritation of the bowels. The discharges are very acrid, and generally their green color indicates acidity. In this case, small doses of magnesia may be repeatedly given. If there are frequent and watery discharges, attended with pain, Dr. Dewees recommends the following preparation ; a tea-spoonful every two hours, until the bowels are more tranquil : Calcined Magnesia, 12 grains ; Laudanum, 3 drops ; Loaf sugar, enough to make it sweet ; Water, quarter of a gill.

If green stools be frequent, a drachm of prepared chalk may be substituted for the magnesia ; or, if there be no fear of diarrhea weakening too much, a scruple of prepared chalk may be *added* to the magnesia ; this is to destroy the acid, and at the same time prevent the lax from being too soon checked. Where the greenness continues without diarrhea, lime-water and milk in equal portions, a tea-spoonful four or five times a day, is often a great advantage.

When the irritating discharges continue, especially if there be streaks of blood, a tea-spoonful of the oil of butter, three or four times a day, is very highly recommended. This is prepared by pouring boiling water on a lump of perfectly sweet butter, stirring it well, to get out the salt, and then skimming off the oil. Gum-arabic water is an extremely valuable remedy.

The best outward application consists of equal parts of borax (borat of soda) and loaf sugar rubbed together, till very fine, and sifted; a small quantity in a dry state to be thrown into the mouth every hour in the day. The child's mouth should not be rubbed with any thing to cleanse it. The practice of scouring it with a piece of flannel is at once useless and cruel. Borax and the mother's milk are sufficient. The infant should take nothing but the breast ; and if the milk be deficient or unhealthy, a fresh nurse should be obtained. The mother should avoid all fermented liquors, vegetables, and other substances likely to sour on the stomach. She may drink freely of rice-water, milk and water, or toast and water.

The utmost attention should be paid to cleanliness Diapers should not be used twice without washing. After every discharge, the irritated parts should be washed in flax-seed tea, and frequently anointed with fresh lard, or some very cooling ointment.

Ulceration of the Mouth.

It usually begins in a small inflamed point, and extends over the gums, and inside of the cheek. Usually accompanied with fever and a restricted state of the bowels. After freely purging with magnesia, until the feverish symptoms disappear, apply the following preparation externally ; touching the ulcerations with it, twice a day, on the point of a camel's hair pencil : Blue vitriol, 10 grains ; Best Peruvian bark, powdered, 1 drachm; Gum arabic, 1 drachm; Honey, 2 drachms; Water, ¾ of a gill; Dissolved and mixed.

Dr. Dewees says this is a speedy cure.

Abscess within the Ear.

Children afflicted with this, generally cry violently, toss their heads about, and complain when the finger is pressed externally against the ear. Their screams are often attributed to colic ; but the remedies for that do no good ; and it is not, like colic, accompanied with wind in the bowels, drawing up of the legs, and coldness of hands and feet. Dr. Dewees recommends the application of a few leeches under the diseased ear, and the introduction of a few drops of laudanum on lint.

When it discharges, it is very important that the parts should be kept clean by frequent washing with fine soap and warm water. After this operation, the canal of the ear may be well bathed with a preparation made of two tea-spoonfuls of lime-water, the same of milk, and twenty drops of the Tincture of Myrrh. This mixture should be prepared fresh every time it is wanted, and thrown into the ear four or five times a day. The child should be made to lie on the diseased side, that the matter may be discharged freely.

If neglected, permanent deafness is sometimes the

result. Where there is a continued succession of them for a long time, an issue is recommended on the arm of the side affected.

Teething.

This usually begins about the age of four months, but is sometimes much later. With some it passes over very lightly ; others suffer so extremely, as to bring on convulsions, and even death. The first symptoms are swelling and hardness of the gums, and the dribbling of saliva from the mouth. The child is disposed to bite every substance he can lay hold of. Sometimes his sleep is feverish and restless, and he has a short, dry cough. The second summer of a child's life is full of perils.

Much trouble and danger might be avoided, if mothers would carefully observe the state of the digestive organs, and regulate diet carefully. If the child nurses, her own food and drink should be very mild and easy of digestion. If weaned, his nourishment should consist of similar articles; for, during teething, there is a constant tendency to disorders of the bowels. After the grinding teeth are formed, food may become more varied and substantial than before ; but still it should principally consist of bread and milk, rice, arrow-root, &c. Small pieces of bread, not recently baked, spread with butter, are safe diet for teething children. If the butter be perfectly sweet, it i. medicinal ; otherwise it had better not be used.

If the child's system is habitually relaxed, use mild astringent food, such as crackers and boiled milk, rice, &c., and demulcent drinks; if it be in a restricted state, let him drink new milk, sweetened with flake manna, or W. I. molasses, and his food consist of articles gently laxative.

Check the indiscreet kindness of friends, who would tempt him with sweetmeats, cakes, fruit, &c. Let his clothing be comfortably warm ; and if the weather be

6

cool, make his shirts of soft flannel. Protect him from morning and evening dews; avoid cold baths, and do not let him long remain wet.

Purgative doses of senna-tea, manna, magnesia, &c. are sometimes necessary. If there is a good deal of inflammation in the bowels, and the discharges are bloody, let them drink gum-arabic water, and take a tea-spoonful of the syrup of white poppies once or twice in the course of twenty-four hours. When the skin is hot and dry, it is a great comfort to have the body sponged with warm water, and wiped with a squeezed sponge. In fine weather, moderate exercise in the open air is salutary. The best thing for the child to bite is a *flat* ivory ring, or a piece of India rubber. The gums should be carefully inspected and rubbed. If they are very much swollen and inflamed, a physician ought to be called to apply the lancet. The operation does little good unless the tooth is distinctly felt by the instrument ; then it affords instant relief, and the pain is exceedingly slight. Sometimes great inflammation and swelling produce convulsive starting and twitching of the fingers : these are certain signs of approaching danger.

Convulsions.

A physician should be called as quick as possible. The child should be immersed in a warm bath, as high as the hips, for ten or fifteen minutes ; and a brisk emetic administered immediately. While the convulsions continue, sprinkle the face with the coldest water that can be obtained. Have every part of the clothing loose. If there is a hard, quick pulse, redness of face, and aversion to the light, a leech ought to be applied to each temple. After the emetic has operated freely, a dose of jalap may be given. If the fits still continue, after the fulness of the system has been reduced by the foregoing measures, they will probably be removed by administering to a child of two years one drop of laudanum and two of essence of peppermint in a tea-spoonful of water every four hours.

Worms.

The symptoms are generally paleness, offensive breath, appetite voracious or diminished, habit of picking the nose, grinding the teeth, a tumid belly, and severe, gnawing pains in the intestines. Children while confined to their mother's milk are not subject to them. The diet ought to be light and easy of digestion. Green vegetables and unripe fruits are very injurious. Those who eat freely of brown bread, and W. I. molasses, are said to be less liable to this complaint. Attention should be paid to air and exercise.

Of all the remedies for worms, none are so highly extolled as the Carolina Pink Root. Take a quantity suitable to the age, and pour upon it half a pint of pretty strong boiling coffee, and let it steep. Pour half of it into a cup with cream and sugar, and let the child drink it in the morning, as if it were real coffee ; the other half may be given at tea time ; bread and butter may be eaten with it, as usual. This should be repeated three days in succession ; on the fourth, should the bowels not be opened, give a dose of castor oil, or senna-tea. Dr. Dewees says, " We have safely prescribed this remedy many hundred times. For children from one year to two, we give but two drachms of Pink Root; for those from two to five, one third of an ounce ; from five to twelve, half an ounce. We do not believe it safe to go beyond those doses ; and we are certain these quantities are sufficient, whenever this plant is the proper remedy. It may be used with perfect safety when fever is present." If the root has been freshly dug, the doses ought to be diminished considerably ; at least until the effects have been tried. It is disguised in coffee merely because children dislike the taste of it very much. Sometimes an infusion is made of a quarter of an ounce of Pink Root with one drachm of powdered senna, steeped in half a pint of boiling water. A child of two years may take a table-spoonful sweetened, twice a day, as long as the symptoms continue; if it operates too powerfully, the rhubarb may be omitted for a while.

Worm-seed oil, made from the seed of Jerusalem Oak, has high reputation, and is more conveniently administered to very young children than the Pink Root. Printed directions accompany each bottle. Sometimes the powdered seed are given mixed with twice their quantity of honey, or syrup; a child of two or three years may take a table-spoonful morning and evening. Sometimes the seed are merely spread on bread and butter. When the expressed juice of the plant is used, a table-spoonful is a common dose for a child of two or three years. It is often necessary to continue it for several days. Where there are feverish symptoms this medicine should not be administered in any form. After taking it, no nourishment should be given for some hours.

The juice of wormwood, with an equal quantity of castor oil, is recommended for worms. A child of twelve years may take a table-spoonful of each.

Different species of worms are affected by different remedies. For the Ascarides, or thread-worm, which cause a very uncomfortable itching about the seat, aloes are considered a remedy. Therefore, twenty drops of elixir proprietatis are often given in a little sweetened milk, morning, noon, and evening, to children from two to four years; and thirty drops to those from five to seven. A tea-spoonful of the elixir in a wine-glass of warm milk, used at bed time, as an injection, two or three times a week, is beneficial.

Whooping Cough.

This begins like a common cold, with hoarseness, short fits of coughing, and some fever. The peculiar whooping sound, which gives its name, sometimes comes on very early, sometimes late, and more rarely not at all. It is about six weeks reaching its height, and the same in declining. Proper attention as soon as the hoarseness begins, would generally prevent the disease from assuming a severe form. Through the whole disorder, the diet should be very low, and free use made of demulcent drinks, like flax-seed tea, slippery elm, &c. W. I. molasses mixed with linseed oil and eaten plentifully on brown bread, is good diet. In the absence of linseed oil, pure sweet oil may be used. All animal food or broths must be avoided. Rennet whey is preferable to milk. Doses of castor oil should be given. After purging, small doses of Ipecacuanha, or syrup of squills, or Coxe's hive syrup, may be given to promote expectoration ; or, if there is great oppression and evident accumulation of phlegm, it should be given in quantities sufficient to vomit. For a child of three or four months, eight drops of the hive syrup every hour or two is enough to promote expectoration: if it is desirable to have it act as an emetic, give the same dose every fifteen minutes. Alter the proportions according to the age of the patient, and the effect produced on different constitutions. Coxe's hive syrup is made thus : Seneca snake-root, bruised; squills, dried and bruised; each half a pound ; water, half a pint. Boil over a slow fire till the water is half consumed ; strain it, and add four pints of strained honey ; boil this to the consistence of syrup, and add sixteen grains of tartar emetic to every pound of it.

This disease is peculiarly troublesome to infants, because they cannot bring up the phlegm, except by vomiting. They should feed only upon their mother's milk, and the bowels be kept open with castor oil.

Some consider whooping cough contagious ; others an epidemic in the air. It is often avoided by change of neighborhood.

Sometimes a chronic cough remains, which may end in permanent debility. Garlic is very highly recommended for this. A child of six or seven years may

6*

begin by taking a third of a common-sized clove, morning, noon, and evening; gradually increasing the dose as the system becomes accustomed to it. One of ten years may begin with half a clove, three times a day; and so on for greater ages.

Change of air is extremely important. To walk or ride out, to go from the city to the country, or from the country to the city, is very desirable. During the first stages, however, when the lungs are easily inflamed, the patient should be kept in a moderate temperature, and not suddenly exposed to cold.

If vaccination has never been performed, it greatly relieves the cough to try it about the sixth week of its progress.

Mumps.

This is a swelling of the glands, sometimes on one cheek, sometimes on both. It increases for three or four days, then lessens, and generally disappears in three or four more. The swelling is hard and slightly painful; generally of little consequence, especially if it be in the warmer season of the year, and unaccompanied with fever. Wash the swelling with a decoction of poppy-heads and chamomile flowers, or warm sweet oil, and keep them warm with flannel. Live low, and use mild purgatives. In case of feverish symptoms, drink a solution of cream of tartar, or other cooling liquids. Great care is necessary about taking cold; for this sometimes occasions the disease to change its place, and produces painful disorders. Should this accident take place, send for a physician.

Croup, or Hives.

This disease is exceedingly dangerous, and often suddenly fatal. A physician should be immediately called; and in the mean time not a moment lost in applying remedies. These ought always to be at hand, where there are children ; for the attack is generally in the night. Fat, florid children are peculiarly subject to it, especially if they live near water, or where the air is cold and moist. It is an inflammation about the wind-pipe, causing a thick mucous membrance very hard to break. It comes on in two ways. 1st. By hoarseness, perceived in the cough, but not in the speech ; the difficulty of breathing, attended with a hissing noise, gradually increases for several days, the face becomes red, the veins of the neck full, the skin hot, &c. 2d. It comes on suddenly and violently, with a shrill, sonorous cough, flushed face, painful labor in breathing, &c.

Dr. Dewees says, " If your inexperienced ear can-not distinguish the shrill, metallic ringing called the 'croupy sound,' instantly proceed upon the supposition that *any* hoarseness may be of the dangerous kind ; especially as the remedies employed for one kind will certainly relieve the other. If appropriate remedies were applied in the forming stage of croup, we have every reason to believe that this formidable complaint could be stopped in nineteen cases out of twenty."

When hoarseness is perceived, inflame the throat by the external application of spirits of turpentine, or hartshorn, or mustard and vinegar—not continued to blistering. When it is removed, cover the throat with flannel, or something warm. At the same time admin-ister, in doses suitable to the age, the compound syrup of squills, or Coxe's hive syrup, as an expectorant ; or, if the breathing be much disturbed, give enough for an emetic.

A tea-spoonful would probable act as an expecto-rant for a child of two years old ; and if repeated a few times at intervals of fifteen minutes, would act as an emetic.

The diet should be very low, confined to barley-water, flax-seed tea, and similar articles. The patient should be kept in an atmosphere of moderate tempera-ture, and care be taken about exposure to the cold, or a draught of air. This *preventative* system is very highly commended by Dr. Dewees, on the strength of his own experience.

In cases of *sudden* and violent attacks, bold remedies must be used, and *whatsoever is done must be done quickly*. The first object is to induce vomiting, and the second, perspiration. The following is the course pursued by an old and experienced physician of Boston, who has been remarkably successful in cases of croup. Apply moistened tobacco to the throat and chest; warm it a little first, if convenient; this will probably induce vomiting. Then steep a long-nine cigar in a cup of hot water; to a child of two years, give a table-spoonful of the liquor, warm, every ten or fifteen minutes, unless it vomit freely without a continued repetition. A child of eight years might take twice the quantity. The nauseating should be continued for twenty-four hours, provided any of the croupy sound remains; because for two or three days this disease is very liable to renew its attacks. Instead of tobacco leaves to the throat and chest, some apply a cloth well covered with goose oil, hen's oil, or fresh lard, and plentifully sprinkled with yellow Scotch snuff; a soft poultice of crumbs, or meal, with a quantity of snuff stirred in, is thought to have still more of the strength of tobacco.

Many are afraid of tobacco, on account of its powerful properties. The experienced physician, already alluded to, declares that he never knew, or heard, of any person's being killed by *swallowing* tobacco; and his assertion is supported by the celebrated Sir Astley Cooper, who says that in the whole course of his immensely extensive practice, he never knew of an individual destroyed in that way. Taken by *injection*, it is very often fatal. An excess of tobacco-tea produces nausea, giddiness, &c.; but these disagreeable effects soon pass away; and they are nothing, compared with the danger of not arresting the croup in season.

To induce perspiration, the feet and legs should be put in warm water, wiped, and well covered with woollen. The child should be put in a warm bed, with his head a little elevated. Warm flax-seed tea, with one or two grains of Ipecac stirred in it, helps both perspiration and expectoration.

Those who do not choose to use tobacco, should induce *speedy* vomiting by giving a child of two years three tea-spoonfuls of the wine of Ipecac. The operation may be assisted with warm water, and a little more Ipecac at short intervals, if necessary.

When the skin becomes moist, and the cough sounds loose, there is no more need of powerful emetics ; but keep up the nausea with warm flax-seed tea, or warm water, with a few grains of Ipecac, as long as there are any remains of the croupy cough.

Some resort to purging as well as vomiting ; but this is wrong. The child's strength becomes so much exhausted by this double process, that there is no power to contend with the disease, and he sometimes dies of weakness. For this reason, if diarrhea comes on in the midst of croup, it should be checked with a few drops of laudanum.

No physic should be given for at least two days ; and strength should be recruited with arrow-root, sago jelly, &c. When the croup is fairly over, if the bowels are at all restricted, give doses of castor oil. Repeat this without fear, once or twice a day, to almost any extent, until it operates. At the same time let the child be nourished with a little chicken broth, or other light food, not astringent. Guard him from exposure to cold, damp air.

The following is recommended by a skilful nurse, who has often tried it very successfully, particularly in the last stages of croup, when a membrane is formed in the throat. Immediately give the patient snuff until it sneezes several times. Into a gill of molasses, a table-spoonful of sweet oil, and the juice of one lemon, stir as much cayenne pepper as is suitable to the age. A child of five years would probably bear a small tea-spoonful. Give a tea-spoonful of this mixture quite often, till it affords relief. If a lemon is not at

hand, use sharp vinegar.   At the same time, cover the
throat, and upper part of the chest, with a flannel well
soaked in goose oil, pig's foot oil, or sweet oil, and
lightly sprinkled over with cayenne.   Apply the warm
bath to the feet, and induce perspiration as above directed, with warm water, or flax-seed tea, mixed with
Ipecac.   Repeat the sneezing quite often.

As it takes some minutes to mix the preparation
mentioned above, it would be well in the mean time to
moisten the throat by pouring down a table-spoonful of
goose oil, sweet oil, or something of the kind.

Succeeding attacks of croup are less violent and dangerous than the first.

Scarlet Fever.

This is frequent, extensive, and very often fatal.
Many think it contagious.   As soon as its presence is
suspected, a physician should be called.   Like other
fevers, it begins with chillness, fulness of the head, lassitude, nausea, &c.   The surface soon becomes red
and hot, the throat and tongue inflamed, and covered
with little points of an intensely deep scarlet blue.   On
the second or third day the skin becomes very hot, sen-
sitive, and covered with a bright red eruption, which
appears first on the neck and face.   It usually continues
about four days.

The worst species of scarlet fever often comes on
very suddenly.   The patient becomes pale, sick, faint,
and giddy.

In its simple form it sometimes passes lightly, with
little medical aid.   The first thing is to administer a
smart emetic of Ipecacuanha.   After free vomiting, use
a brisk dose of castor oil, or magnesia.   From time to
time give mild diaphoretics ; as a few grains of Ipecac
stirred in warm flax-seed tea.   The diet should be very
low ; all mixtures of animal food, spices, and liquors
fermented or distilled, should be carefully avoided.

Some time after purging with castor oil, a dose of

salts may be given.   When there is pain in the head, and the pulse is full and hard, physicians always resort to bleeding.   If the fever continues to run high, emetics may be repeated.   When the skin is hot and dry, sponging with cool vinegar and water is comforting; but if this produces chillness, use warm water only.   If the eruption takes place imperfectly, or suddenly recedes, the warm bath is highly recommended.

An infusion made of a tea-spoonful of cayenne pepper, steeped an hour in a pint of boiling water, stirred and strained, is much praised as a gargle, appropriate to the first stages of the disease, when the throat is not ulcerated.

To cleanse foul ulcers in the throat, emetics are recommended, followed by a gargle made of a tea-spoonful, or less, of Muriatic acid in a gill of water, either with or without honey.   If the child is too young to gargle, the throat is syringed.

The favorable symptoms of scarlet fever are, slower pulse, decreasing heat and redness, and the return of refreshing sleep.   The danger is generally considered over after the ninth day.   During convalescence, the diet should continue very low.   The room should be kept cool from the beginning ; warmth increases the headache and fever.

This disease is often followed by dropsical affections. This ought to be relieved by purging, and saline diuretics, as nitre and squills.   Children between three and seven years may take one fourth of a grain of squills, mixed with eight grains of nitre, three or four times a day.   Those between seven and fifteen years may take twelve grains of nitre with half a grain of squills.   Bloodletting is sometimes necessary.

Measles.

These begin like a cold, with hoarseness, difficult breathing, drowsiness, inflamed eyes, and considerable fever.   Sneezing almost always attends this complaint. In a few days, small red spots, perceptible to the touch, appear on the face and neck, and spread over the body; about the fifth day they usually turn pale brown, and on the eighth or ninth disappear. Unlike other eruptive complaints, the fever increases with the eruption. Scarlet fever is the only disease for which it can be mistaken; but it is distinguished from that by sneezing, watery eyes, severe cough, and an eruption less vivid in color. Measles are attended with inflammatory symptoms; sometimes highly so. For this reason, the common practice of giving heating teas, wine-whey, milk-punch, &c., to throw out the eruption, is often injurious. It ought to disappear on the eighth or ninth day, in the course of nature. If it abruptly disappears, two or three days after it comes, it is a bad sign; especially if it be attended by severe vomiting, or diarrhea. It is a very general custom to use snake-root and saffron-tea, to send out the eruptions on such occasions; but Dr. Bigelow says it is better to bring them back with diaphoretic, or even emetic doses of ipecac, in warm flax-seed-tea; this is probably recommended because it is certain not to increase the fever. Warm baths are good to bring out the eruption. The best thing to prevent the measles from striking in, is to guard the patient from any current of air, and keep the darkened room of a moderate and equal degree of warmth. Dr. Dewees says, "It should not exceed sixty-four or five degrees; sixty, perhaps, would be the best standard. It is never proper to keep the patient hot, by either a heated atmosphere or bed-clothes." It is not advisable to cool the skin by sponging, because it is apt to increase the cough.

Castor oil, or senna-tea, given in doses to operate freely. The diet should be very low, and without the slightest mixture of animal juices, spices, wine, &c. The drink should consist entirely of such things as gum arabic water, flax-seed-tea, barley-water, &c.

To appease the cough that always attends measles, the pectoral syrup may be used, or a little paragoric in flax-seed-tea. For small children, the syrup of poppies is much recommended. It may be given in the night or day, as necessity arises ; a tea-spoonful is sufficient for an infant six months old ; a dessert-spoonful for one of two years. The cough sometimes continues after all other symptoms have disappeared. This must not be neglected, even if it be not severe ; for the result is often fatal. The diet should be strictly confined to milk and vegetables for some time after recovering from measles : great care should be taken about exposure to cold or damp; and in cold, or cool weather, flannel should be worn next to the skin. Pectoral syrup, flax-seed-tea, and similar things loosening to the cough, may be given; and if the state of the system requires it, gentle laxatives should be used.

The measles is an epidemic disease, much milder some seasons than others. Experienced mothers sometimes carry their children through it, without medical aid ; yet this is a daring practice ; for it is a complaint of which very many die. Dr. Dewees attributes this fatality, in a great measure, to the use of heating teas, and stimulating articles to bring out the eruption, and to a want of care in keeping the diet very mild and low during recovery.

When the eruption comes out imperfectly in the beginning, when the spots are pale, and there is a good deal of fever, it is very unfavorable.

When the eruption strikes in, with shivering, or delirium, the danger is very great.

Nettle Rash.

This is very apt to attack teething children. It is a florid eruption accompanied with a very stinging sensation. The fever and itching both increase toward night. It is very apt to arise from taking acids ; such as green fruit, cabbage and vinegar, lemonade when the body is heated, &c.

It is common to give salts for this disease ; but they are decidedly injurious. Magnesia should be freely prescribed, because the intention is to counteract acid :

7

taken by itself, or mixed with rhubarb, it is the most proper and certain purgative. Lime-water and milk may also be given, particularly when the eruption has continued several days. Milk diet should be adhered to, and no solid food taken. If there be no fever, chicken tea and beef tea may be given. Plain water, or toast and water, not too cold, are the best drinks. Lemonade is sometimes given, but the effect is very bad.

To relieve the itching, rye or wheat flour may be rubbed on. Soap, rubbed on with the moistened finger, or sponge, is a great relief.

If the eruption all disappears suddenly, it often produces serious consequences, though it is rarely fatal. Warm snake-root and saffron tea should be given immediately ; the patient should be covered in bed ; and if the feet and legs be cold, put them into warm water with mustard in it.

Inflammation of the Throat.

This comes on with huskiness, and next with pain and inflammation. When recent and mild, flannel, or a stocking bound on warm from the foot, will often cure it. A tea-spoonful of salt, and a sprinkle of cayenne stirred in a tumbler of cold water, and used half at a time, every hour in the day, is an excellent gargle. After the throat becomes very sore, it is better to use warm gargles of sage tea, honey and water, vinegar and water, &c. It is well to inflame the throat by the outward application of spirits of turpentine, or mustard and vinegar. When there is a good deal of fever, emetics and cathartics should be administered ; and sometimes blood-letting is necessary.

This disease is almost always occasioned by taking cold. Some are peculiarly liable to it, particularly after they have once had it. Washing the throat every morning with cold water is said to be a preventive ; and gargling with water that has alum dissolved in it is much recommended for the same purpose.

Diarrhea.

Many have been killed by using powerful astringents to check this disease in its first stages. The cause should always be removed by the use of cathartics. An acid state of the stomach is indicated by frequent and light green discharges, with curdled milk, sour eructations, &c. ; in this case, magnesia is the best physic. In bilious diarrhea, or " summer complaint," the discharges are apt to be bright yellow ; if so, purge with castor oil ; if they are frequent and green, use magnesia and rhubarb. Rennet-whey, both as food and drink, answers an admirable purpose in bilious diarrhea.

For mucous discharges, often produced by sudden check of perspiration, improper use of the cold bath, &c., give castor oil and rhubarb tea, in laxative rather than purgative doses.

Where a good deal of pain and fever attend, castor oil is the best physic, given in appropriate doses every two hours till it operates freely. The occasional use of the warm bath is likewise recommended, to allay the fever.

In some cases, diarrhea is produced by worms. Where this is suspected, anthelmintics should be administered.

During the whole course of diarrhea, of every kind, great attention should be paid to diet. But little food should be taken, and none of a solid kind. Water-gruel, thick gum arabic water, &c. are the proper articles ; the latter is particularly good to allay inflammation. Drink should be avoided, and the face and hands often sponged with cool water. The lips may be occasionally moistened with flax-seed tea, barley-water, &c.

The oil of butter is very salutary and soothing in most stages of chronic diarrhea. [*For the manner of preparing this, see Baby's Sore Mouth, p.* 51.]

Tea made of fresh lamb-suet, and sweetened with loaf sugar, has often been found very healing and nutritious in the last stages of diarrhea, when the stomach re-

jected almost every kind of food.   A tea-spoonful may
be given at once, and increased as the patient can
bear it.

Nursing children should be kept entirely upon breast
milk ; if lately weaned, restoration to it will greatly
contribute to recovery.   If the milk is suspected to
be unhealthy, procure a fresh nurse.   The child ought
not to nurse frequently ; especially if the diarrhea be
accompanied with much fever, or there be a coagulum of milk discharged.

When the stomach is acid, very little milk should be
given at any age, unless it be diluted with lime-water.
Of these, mixed in equal portions, a tea-spoonful every
hour or two may be given to an infant of six months,
and two or three times as much to older children.

After the bowels have been thoroughly purged, if
there be no fever, and the patient still continues restless
and in pain, paregoric or laudanum may be used at night,
to induce sleep.   Sometimes it is necessary to mix it
with injections.   If the feet and legs are cold, woollen
stockings should be put on ; and it may be well to rub
them, after bathing in warm mustard and water.   If the
bowels are cold, they should be often rubbed with the
bare warm hand, and covered with flannel.   The child
should not sit on cold painted floors, or marble steps,
or stand in a current of air.

When decidedly recovering, boiled rice may be eaten
with sugar and nutmeg : a little chicken tea may be
taken, or a small piece of ham sucked.

Children habitually troubled with weak, cold bowels,
accompanied with frequent diarrhea, should eat white
bread and crackers, rice, &c.   Their food and medicines should be sweetened with loaf sugar.   If molasses
be used, it should be sugar baker's.   The milk they
eat should be boiled.   They should drink but little,
and that of bland, demulcent articles, like flax-seed tea,
low-mallows tea, gum arabic water, warm milk and molasses, &c.   Milk thoroughly warmed with a hot iron,
after the manner of making flip, is excellent for a re-

laxed state of the bowels. An admirable medicine for such cases is an equal portion of castor oil and paregoric ; children of two years may take a tea-spoonful at a time, till it operates sufficiently. Diarrhea ought never to be neglected, especially in hot weather, and the cool of autumn.

Cholera Infantum.

A dangerous disease, requiring the early advice of physicians. It sometimes comes on as simple diarrhea, and sometimes with vomiting, purging, and spasms, like cholera morbus. The eyes are fierce, or languid, and in sleep half closed. Thirst is intense, but water is vomited as soon as drank. To appease the child, it is best to give a tea-spoonful at a time, as warm as convenient. Gentle purgatives are generally employed in preference to emetics ; especially castor oil. If medicine cannot be retained by reason of violent vomiting, nothing is so certain, or so prompt, as an injection of a gill of warm water, in which a large tea-spoonful of common salt is dissolved : this is for a child a year old, and upward, proportionably less for younger.

However frequent the discharges may be, the injection must be given. Should it not bring anything off, it must be repeated, and an attempt made to force it high into the bowels; or, should the vomiting continue, it must again be tried in half an hour. Dr. Dewees says, " We have a hundred times seen this simple plan give entire relief." The virtue of the injection depends on the salt. A tea-spoonful of strong coffee, without sugar or milk, every fifteen minutes, has great power to tranquilize the stomach. It should especially be given to very young children ; but all ages would profit by it in larger doses. When the legs and feet are cold, they are rubbed with warm vinegar and mustard, or cayenne, until the skin be inflamed. When some parts of the body are parching hot, and others

7*

very cold, blisters are recommended, and frequent warm baths.

These things are mentioned in case a doctor cannot be obtained ; but medical aid should be sought, by all means.

This disease may be brought on by too early weaning ; and restoration to the breast will sometimes effect a cure. The child must not be allowed to satisfy his thirst by sucking too much, or too often.

Those who do not nurse should be fed exclusively on rice-water and milk, barley-water, and gum arabic-water, during the first stages ; and afterwards with very thin arrow-root, sago, or rice. When no fever is present, a very little piece of ham, or salt fish, may be allowed. The drinks should consist of balm-tea, marsh-mallows tea, or water with toasted bread in it. Worsted stockings, and flannel next to the skin, are recommended ; and if the child is teething, the gums should be lanced when they appear swollen and inflamed.

The sovereign remedy is change of air. If not too early in the season, remove from the city to the country. At all events let the child ride out often, and, if possible, cross a river, when the weather is suitable.

Vomiting.

The most healthy babies will often throw up curdled milk, because the process of digestion naturally produces this change. But if they throw it up a few minutes after receiving it, especially if they continue to do so repeatedly, it is a sign of an acid stomach, and it sometimes becomes necessary to attend to it. For children under a year, a tea-spoonful of lime-water, and as much milk, once an hour, will generally be sufficient. If the bowels be loose, the following mixture may be given, a tea-spoonful every hour or two ; a tea-spoonful of calcined magnesia in eight or ten tea-spoonfuls of water or milk, with three or four drops of laudanum, and a little sugar. If the child be costive, the laudanum must be omitted. An injection of salt and water will almost always stop incessant vomiting. (*See Cholera Infantum, p.*69.)

When children vomit merely from an overloaded stomach, or the use of improper food, it should be encouraged with warm water, or warm chamomile tea, till the offending substance is removed. After this, an injection is sometimes necessary.

Colic.

Usually occasioned by wind, or by the mother's eating improper food. The child moans, or laughs, in its sleep ; wakes suddenly; cries out violently; and, when in great pain, draws its limbs up toward its body. Warm catnip tea sweetened, or an infusion of carroway or fennel seed are in common use on such occasions. But a much better remedy is the following:—Boil a tea-spoonful of mustard-seed with a crust of toasted bread in half a pint of water, about half an hour. Sweeten it, and give as many tea-spoonfuls of the liquid as the child seems to desire. If the pain arises from wind, this will soon quiet it.

When the child throws up curdled milk soon after it is swallowed, and its bowels are restricted, half a tea-spoonful of magnesia, stirred in warm catnip-tea, is beneficial.

Restricted State of the System.

When the colic is accompanied with costiveness and heat, small doses of warm sweet oil, or castor oil, may be safely repeated every hour or two, till they produce effect. In obstinate cases, laxative injections are necessary. For babes, a suppository of soap is often useful. This consists of a round piece of hard soap, about as big as a quill, tapering to a point ; to be dipped in warm water, sweet oil, or fresh lard, and applied like an injection pipe. Sometimes it is a relief to rub the bowels gently with warm flannel, or rub on a little camphorated spirits with the warm hand.

Children troubled with restricted habits should often eat soft rye hasty-pudding, or wheat mush, with W. I. molasses. Very warm W. I. molasses and water is gently laxative, and if taken when going to bed, produces perspiration. It is an excellent remedy for small children that have taken cold and are feverish. New milk, sweetened with W. I. molasses, is mildly laxative and nutritious, and is a very good regulator when the bowels are in any way out of order. Taken freely, it often does perceptible good, when the stomach rejects more active medicines.

Rickets.

The most common symptoms are the head unusually large, bones growing crooked, countenance grave, flesh soft and loose, and appetite feeble. Some weakly children have a predisposition to it. But it is generally brought on by want of nourishment ; indigestible or fermented food ; want of exercise, and pure air ; lying in wet cradles with foul clothing ; or the frequent use of opiate medicines and spirituous liquors.

Its cure depends more upon nursing than medicine ; though doses of rhubarb are sometimes necessary. The child should be gently exercised in the arms, and cheerfulness encouraged by play. Its limbs should be frequently rubbed with the warm hand, and with the essence of wormwood. Cold bathing is good, if it can be borne; but discontinue it the moment it seems injurious. The open air, in fine weather, is very beneficial ; but extremes of heat and cold should be carefully avoided. The clothing should be merely comfortable; for perspiration and chills both tend to increase the disorder. The food should be dry and nourishing ; such as rice, toasted bread, chickens, conserve of roses, &c. Tonics, such as wormwood-tea, or Peruvian bark, night and morning, have an excellent effect, if children can be persuaded to take them.

Dropsy in the Head.

This complaint is often produced by unnaturally forcing the intellect of children, from the unpardonable vanity of having them appear as prodigies. It likewise originates in various other causes. The first symptoms are fretfulness and debility. The child leaves his toys, and goes somewhere to recline his head; he shuns light, and is averse to motion ; one or both his cheeks are flushed, his tongue is furred, and there is a frequent inclination to vomit. As the disorder proceeds, he rubs his head on the pillow, squints, moans, and starts in his sleep ; and his eyes assume a brilliant, glassy appearance. As soon as you suspect the presence of this disease, send for a skilful doctor with all speed. I have heard of one child, given over by the physicians, whose life was thought to be saved, by having his head shaved, covered with a poultice of onions slightly stewed in vinegar, and his feet bathed in warm water with mustard in it.

Inflammation of the Eyes.

Sometimes from about the fourth to the eighth day after birth, the eyes become inflamed and swelled, and are found glued up in the morning. If neglected in this state, blindness may be the consequence. At the first washing, plenty of water should be used about the eyes. If they become inflamed, bathe them gently with the mucilage of sassafras, or a lukewarm decoction of poppy heads. The mother's milk, frequently milked upon them, is thought to be very useful in preventing their sticking together. The pulp of rotten apples laid on the eyelids when the child is asleep, takes down the inflammation, applied as cold as it can be without occasioning a start. Of course, the babe should be kept turned away from the sunshine, and all bright lights. In bad cases, it is necessary to apply small leeches.

Involuntary Diuretic Discharges.

Where this is the disease of habit, patient care should be taken to correct it, by teaching the child to attend to his natural wants at stated seasons ; particularly the last thing at night. Punishment ought not to be inflicted, because it often arises from disease. Fresh air, moderate exercise, and frequent bathing in cold water, are good. Sleep on a straw bed, or mattrass, wear flannel next the skin, and frequently rub the whole person with a stiff brush. Eat nourishing, but not stimulating food, and avoid drink as much as possible. A plaster of Burgundy pitch, applied very low on the back, is recommended. From three to ten drops of the oil of rosemary in a spoonful of water, taken when going to bed, is thought serviceable. Instead of this, some use a decoction of white oak bark ; being very astringent, it should be given in moderate doses, and discontinued when the effects are too severe.

In obstinate cases, a child of two years, if not weakly, may take four drops of the tincture of cantharides, three times a day, in a table-spoonful of sweetened water. Older children may take ten or twelve drops. This may be cautiously increased, unless it produce a sensation of heat in the diuretic discharges ; in that case, it must be stopped. If stranguary ensue, give flaxseed-tea or gum arabic water; if severe, add a few grains of camphor, and a few drops of laudanum.

It is recommended to bathe the loins, and seat of the kidneys, twice a day, with spirits of turpentine, and spirits of hartshorn, a tea-spoonful of each mixed with an ounce of soap liniment.

Burns.

Accidents of this kind are so common, that remedies ought always to be in the house. Take any portion of linseed oil, or sweet oil, and stir lime-water into it, till it is as stiff as you wish to spread on a cloth. Apply it as soon as possible. In common cases, nothing will be necessary but to renew it occasionally. This is one of the safest and best remedies for burns.

Bathing freely in sweet oil, and covering the burn with cotton wool, is considered an excellent thing to take the fire out. Sometimes it is difficult to make young children endure this. The constant application of cold vinegar and water will often take out the inflammation, especially if it be not very extensive; and it is very comforting to the little sufferer. When burns are exceedingly painful, immediately after they are inflicted, nothing gives so much relief as cold applications. Sometimes ice and water is laid on in a bladder.

When the burn is blistered, spirits of turpentine a little warmed is recommended. Care should be taken not to apply the turpentine to the sound skin; and if the burn be considerable, the air should be excluded as quick as possible. The first dressing may remain on ten or twelve hours; and when taken off, care must be taken not to expose it to the cold. Basilicon ointment is good for the second dressing the blisters being first opened with the point of a needle. Should the surrounding parts be much inflamed, bread and milk poultice had better be used till it subsides; then return to the Basilicon ointment, or simple cerate. Should the discharge be too abundant, add a little prepared chalk to the simple cerate.

Burns, in healing, shoot up a kind of jelly-like fungus. It is good to sprinkle burnt alum powdered around the edges of this; dry lint is useful, where it can be borne. Care should be taken to separate toes and fingers with bandages, lest they grow together.

When the patient complains of being chilly, free doses of laudanum should be given, and the atmosphere be kept of a moderate temperature. Great care is necessary about taking cold in the burn. All stimulating liquor and animal food should be carefully withheld. Sometimes even bleeding and purging are necessary.

When children cannot obtain sleep, gentle opiates may be given.

Drowning, &c.

To recover persons apparently drowned, the principal object is to *restore natural warmth,* by hot and stimulating applications.

Carry the body in as natural a posture as possible, and be careful not to have the head hang down.   Strip off the wet clothes instantly, and rub the skin with coarse cloths made hot.   Prepare a warm bed as quick as you can, and place the person in it, with his head elevated. Hot cloths and warm bricks should be frequently applied to the bowels and feet ; or, what is still better, a brand suddenly quenched and done up in flannel.   The spine of the back, pit of the stomach, arms, and palms of the hands, should be rubbed with warm brandy, or vinegar, with a little cayenne sprinkled in it.   Snuff or ginger blown up the nose.   The temples chafed with camphorated spirits ; and hartshorn held to the nose. A strong person may hold his nostrils and blow his breath into the patient's mouth with all his force ; if the chest rises, desist from blowing, and press the breast and belly, so as to expel the air again: this operation may be repeated, in imitation of natural breathing.   If this does not succeed, blow through one of the nostrils, keeping the other close.

While these things are being done, a very warm bath should be prepared : if there are no conveniences for this, the body should be covered with warm ashes, or salt, or sand, heated.

While the patient is senseless, it is dangerous to pour liquor into the mouth; but the lips and tongue may be frequently moistened, with warm brandy, or other strong spirits.   As soon as they can swallow, a little warm wine and water may be occasionally given.

It is considered safer to induce vomiting by tickling the throat with an oiled feather, than by emetics.   Strong tea of sage, or chamomile flowers, is recommended; likewise warm water, with a little salt in it.

Warm and stimulating applications should be continued for some time after life returns. If there be oppression, with cough and feverishness, bleeding is necessary; and pectoral syrup, or flax-seed tea, with a few grains of ipecac in it, may be given to loosen the cough.

Similar means should be taken to recover persons who suddenly lose life by a fall, fits, or other accidents. Bleeding, friction, warm bath, outward heat, blowing into the lungs, &c., should be tried, and long persevered in.

Vaccination.

No parents ought to neglect to have their children vaccinated. It is a safe way of escaping a very great danger. It is always desirable to have physicians perform vaccination, because they have opportunities to obtain fresh matter from healthy patients, and can best judge whether it takes thoroughly. But if parents are so situated that a doctor cannot be called, they may perform the operation without the least risk. If any person in the vicinity has the kine-pox, obtain the matter by opening one of the pustules with the point of a needle, on the eighth or ninth day. Slightly scratch the upper part of the arm or leg, in two places so as to bring blood; apply the matter on a little lint, and bind it on. It will rarely fail to produce the eruption in three or four days.

When children are vaccinated they should be entirely free from eruptions of the skin; on this account as well as the absence of all fear, infancy is a good period for the operation. It may be safely performed any time after a babe is four weeks old. It usually passes lightly, and no particular care is necessary concerning diet.

If, by unpardonable neglect, children have the small-

8

pox in its natural and dangerous form, the symptoms
will be drowsiness, loss of appetite, alternate fits of
heat and cold, pain in the head and loins, sudden start-
ings in sleep, and, about the third day, pimples on the
forehead and wrists. Send directly for a physician.
In the mean time keep the patient cool, and give a
simple dose of senna, or Glauber's salts. During the
progress of the disease the food and drink should be
simple and cooling. Wash the mouth, teeth and
throat often with water or vinegar and water. Have plenty of fresh air ; keep the bowels open with mild laxatives; and when the disease has run its course, give purgative doses of rhubarb and senna.

Bleeding at the Nose.

This discharge generally does a great deal of good,
and no means should be taken to stop it, unless it continues so excessive that the lips become pale, the pulse
low, and the extremities cold. In this case, the patient
should be seated nearly upright, with his head a little
reclining; his feet, legs, and hands, should be kept in
luke-warm water ; cold iron, or some cold substance,
applied between the shoulders, and bandages tied pretty
tight about the upper part of the arm, and above the
calf of the leg. As the bleeding diminishes, these
should be gradually slackened and taken away. Sometimes lint, or small pieces of sponge, dipped in strong
spirits of wine, or brandy, are put in the nostrils, and
suffered to remain, till they fall of their own accord.
Cold vinegar and water, or salt and water, may be drank
occasionally. When lying down, the head should be
elevated, and there should be nothing tight about the
neck. A bladder of iced water, or the application of
very cold water, for some time, very far below the
bowels, will usually stop the worst bleeding at the nose.
Ten drops of elixir vitriol, in a wine-glass of water,
taken every hour, is good. If the disease is habitual,
it may be taken twice a day for a month ; and in case

of costiveness, three or four grains of pill cochiæ may be given daily.

Obstructions in the Nose and Throat.

If a child swallows a bean, or any thing of that kind, clap him smartly on the back, and make him sneeze with snuff, ginger, or pepper. The same means may be taken if a bean is in the nose; and grease may be applied outwardly. If more dangerous substances are swallowed, such as brass buttons, needles, pins, &c., it is best to call a doctor. Large pieces of bread, fruit, &c. had better be pushed down, because they will be digested; but cork, wood, bone, metal, &c. should be extracted if possible. Strong rennet-water helps to dissolve some indigestible substances that have been swallowed. If the substance be not hooked, or sharp-pointed, it is well to give a brisk emetic of ipecac, or tobacco tea, and tickle the throat with a feather. Children should be taught to chew their food well, and never witness the dangerous example of putting pins in the mouth.

If infants breathe and nurse with difficulty, on account of obstructions occasioned by a cold, rub the nose at bed-time with fresh lard, or sweet oil.

NOTE. Measles and whooping-cough are epidemics that generally go through families and neighborhoods. Their visitations are apt to be lightest between the ages of 4 and 10 years; and as people never have them but once, parents consider it wise not to screen their children from them, at this period. Scarlet fever usually goes through families wherever it enters; but the same individual very rarely has it twice in a severe form. It is too dangerous not to be avoided, if possible.

COMMON MEDICINES.

(Appropriate doses for children are mentioned in a separate article, beginning p. 43.)

Every family ought to keep a chest of common medicines, such as ipecac, castor oil, magnesia, paregoric, &c.; *and especially such remedies as are useful in croup.* This precaution may be the means of saving life, when a doctor or apothecary cannot be summoned immediately.

All medicines should be kept well covered from the air and light, and have names written on them. All dry substances should be marked with the number of grains they weigh; so that proper doses can be easily given on short notice.

All such things as opium, laudanum, nitric acid, &c. should be kept out of the reach of children ; and by all means marked, in large letters, *Poison*, or *Dangerous.*

The operation of medicine is always favored by very simple food, very sparingly used. Gruel is the best article. As a general rule it is better to avoid the use of emetics, when cathartics will answer the purpose equally well.

There are various circumstances that should modify the doses of medicine. Children and old people cannot bear so much as those of middle age. Infants require much less than children. The constitutions of some individuals are peculiar, and certain medicines affect them more powerfully than others. Feeble persons should take smaller doses than those who are strong. Women in general are affected by less quantities of medicine than men. The inexperienced had better give moderate doses, till effects are tested—except in such emergencies as severe croup, poison, &c. The following tables are merely given to assist the judgment.

Apothecaries' Weight.

20 grains make one scruple.   Ə
3 scruples one drachm.   ʒ
8 drachms one ounce.   ℥
12 ounces one pound.   ℔

If a person from 21 to 40 may take 1 drachm.
A person from 7 to 14 may take   ½ a dr.
From 4 to 7   ⅓ dr. or 1 scruple.
Of four years   ¼ dr. or 15 grains.

Some powders weigh more than others, of course no accurate rule can be given to take them by measure ; but in general terms it may be said that 20 *grains of powder are equivalent to about a tea-spoonful.* In powerful medicines, it is of course imprudent to trust to conjecture.

Castor Oil.

A mild cathartic producing little pain ; therefore best adapted to cases of irritation and inflammation. Recommended to pregnant women, and those lately delivered. Considered the best and safest cathartic for children. One fluid ounce, which is about a quarter of a gill, is the common dose for a grown person. It is sometimes given floating on the surface of mint, or cinnamon water, to disguise the taste. Some think it less disagreeable if mixed with a cup of hot sweetened coffee.

This oil is made from the Palmi Christi, or castor bean. It is commonly expressed ; but it is said to be a better method to shell and skin the beans, boil them in water, and skim the oil off as it rises. Thus prepared, it is clear and sweet, without bad taste or smell, and less liable to become rancid.

Carbonate of Magnesia.

A very good remedy when an acid state of the
8*

stomach is indicated by sour breath and head-ache. A heaped up table-spoonful, well mixed in water or milk, may be taken.

Calcined magnesia is preferred as less apt to produce flatulence. Good for the heart-burn. From half a drachm to two drachms may be taken. The habit of chewing it very frequently is injurious. If the stomach is not acid, a little currant juice, or lemonade, will be necessary to render it cathartic.

It counteracts the salivating properties of calomel, without diminishing other effects. If ten grains of calomel are likely to produce this result, a tea-spoonful of magnesia may be given an hour after, and repeated at intervals of two hours. If there are not free discharges in the course of four hours, larger doses of magnesia may be given, or castor oil taken.

Manna.

A mild agreeable laxative, that may be safely administered to children and the aged. In some constitutions it is apt to induce flatulence ; this may be remedied by the addition of a little cinnamon water, or other aromatic. The dose for a grown person is an ounce, or an ounce and a half ; but, on account of its great mildness, it is generally given mixed with senna, rhubarb, or some other cathartic.

Senna.

If good, the leaves will be of a lively yellowish green, a faint disagreeable smell, and bitterish, nauseous taste. It is somewhat diuretic, and is a prompt, efficient, and safe purgative ; well calculated for cases where a decided, but not very violent impression is desired. Some aromatic is usually combined with it, to render it less painful. 1 ounce of senna leaves, 1 drachm of bruised coriander seed, and a pint of boiling water ; *steeped* an hour in an earthen vessel, and strained ;

dose about a gill. This infusion should often be made fresh, as exposure to the air increases its griping effects. Boiling it has the same tendency.

The following recipe is said to increase its operation, and render it less painful. ½ ounce of senna ; 1 ounce of manna ; 1 ounce of sulphate of magnesia ; 1 drachm of fennel, or coriander seed ; half a pint of boiling water ; *steeped* till it cools. One third given for a dose, and repeated every four or five hours till it operates.

A compound infusion, at once refrigerant and laxative, therefore calculated for feverish complaints, is sometimes made hus :—Senna leaves 1 drachm ; preserved tamarinds 1 ounce ; bruised coriander seed 1 drachm ; brown sugar ½ an ounce ; boiling water half a pint ; *steeped*, and occasionally stirred, four hours in an earthen vessel, not glazed with lead ; strained. Dose from half a gill to a gill.

Rhubarb.

At once a tonic and cathartic. From five to ten grains operate as a laxative and stomachic ; from twenty to thirty as a purgative. Its medicinal properties are peculiar, being both cathartic and astringent. The latter effect follows the former; hence the stomach is left more braced and invigorated than with other physic. An infusion is much used for women, children, and people of delicate constitutions. In costive states of the body, its astringent qualities should be counteracted by mixing it with an equal proportion of soap. Roasting, or long boiling, diminishes its laxative qualities, while the astringent remain ; this is sometimes done in cases of obstinate diarrhea. As a general rule, it is not a good medicine where inflammation exists. It is used in dyspepsia accompanied with costiveness, in chronic dysentery, and the secondary stages of cholera infantum. Equal portions of rhubarb and magnesia are very beneficial in bilious diarrhea, where there is any evidence of acidity. Rhubarb is second only to calomel in its

power of changing to a natural color the very discolor-
ed evacuations common in such disorders; a result
which is considered most desirable. Ten or twelve
grains of rhubarb, mixed with eight or ten grains of
super sulphate of potash is a mild and efficient purgative, that will generally remove ordinary disorders of
the bowels.

Two grains of powdered rhubarb, one grain of ipecacuanha, and two grains of soap, form an excellent tonic
pill for dyspepsia : it is laxative, and leaves the stomach
braced. One may be taken two or three times a day.

The common infusion is made by steeping a drachm
of sliced rhubarb an hour in half a pint of boiling water.
Dose from a quarter of a gill to half a gill ; taken every
three or four hours till it operates. Carroway seed, or
cinnamon, sometimes steeped with it, to diminish its
griping effects. It is often taken in powder, or chewed.
It is an expensive medicine. The Turkey rhubarb,
specked with white, is less apt to excite vomiting, than
that which is entirely deep yellow.

Jalap.

An active cathartic, operating briskly and often pain-
fully. Given in most cases where physic is required ;
particularly applicable in cases of dropsy, being an active diuretic. The aqueous extract, operates moderately, without much griping. The alcoholic extract,
called resin of jalap, operates powerfully, and sometimes severely. From fifteen to thirty grains of the
powder is a dose for a strong grown person, usually
rubbed up with sugar. If taken in flax-seed tea, its
effects are less irritating.

Ten grains of powdered rhubarb, and ten grains of
jalap powder, are a common cathartic, given in molasses, after an emetic has ceased operating, and the
stomach needs to be more thoroughly cleansed.

Aloes.

A warm, stimulating purgative. It quickens the circulation, and is particularly serviceable to persons of phlegmatic habits, weak stomachs, and sedentary life. Two or three grains operate as a laxative ; ten grains is the medium dose ; but it may be augmented to twenty, according to circumstances. It is injurious to bilious habits, and the piles, on account of its tendency to inflame the bowels. Considered improper during pregnancy, and for those troubled with bleeding at the lungs. It is recommended for thread-worms ; and has been used as an emmenagogue. Soccatrine aloes are considered the best.

Sulphate of Iron.

An approved emmenagogue. One drachm in a gill of rose-water. A tea-spoonful taken at eleven and four o'clock every day. At the same time, take every night one or two pills, made of pulverized aloes and myrrh, each one drachm ; divided into thirty pills. Continue this till the healthful operations of nature are restored. Wear warm drawers, woollen stockings, and flannel next the skin. Cast aside stays and tight clothing. Often bathe the feet in warm water, and cover them with woollen during the night.

Anderson's Pills.

These are composed of aloes, jalap, and oil of aniseed. An old-fashioned and safe family medicine. Good for a restricted state of the system ; for common colds where physic is needed ; and for debilitated state of the stomach in the spring. A very weak person might take one ; two is a common dose ; and three if a decided effect is desirable.

Dinner Pills.

Made of aloes, mastich, red roses, and syrup of wormwood. Convenient for travellers troubled with restricted habits. Two or three may be taken half an hour before dinner. Safe and not inconvenient in their effects.

Salts.

An ounce of Epsom salts is a dose for a strong person. A sailor just returned from sea, or one exposed to bad diet or air, may take it with advantage. Half an ounce is usually a sufficient cathartic for delicate constitutions. It is peculiarly adapted to cutaneous eruptions, whether from humors, or contact with poison; in such cases it is recommended to be taken occasionally, while external applications are made. Full-blooded people sometimes take it two or three times a week in the spring, to cool the blood, in doses of two or three tea-spoonfuls dissolved in water, early in the morning.

It is entirely unsuited to all cases of dysentery, diarrhea, &c.

Some prefer Rochelle salts, as being less bitter and disagreeable. They operate better, if considerable water be drank at the same time.

Pill Rufi.

A safe and cheap cathartic. Quite a large lump can be bought for twenty-five cents. Softened by warmth, it can be made into pills about the size of a pea, of which from one to four may be taken at night, according to its effects.

Picra.

Soccatrine aloes one pound; white canella three ounces; separately powdered and mixed. Apothecaries sell it already prepared, under the name of hiera picra powder. One or two tea-spoonfuls may be taken in molasses. It is considered a good cathartic for the aged, because it does not reduce their strength. People may eat as usual. A tincture is often made by bottling an ounce of the powder in a pint of rum ; half a wine-glass is a dose. A prudent fear of evil habits will prevent the wise from mixing their medicines with ardent spirit.

Elixir Proprietatis.

One ounce of saffron, one ounce of myrrh, and one ounce of aloes. Pulverize them ; steep the myrrh in half a pint of brandy, or N. E. rum, for four days ; then add the saffron and aloes. Let it stand in the sunshine, or a warm place, for a fortnight, and shake it once or twice a day. At the end of a fortnight, fill up the bottle with brandy or rum, and let it stand a month. It is a useful family medicine when the digestive powers are out of order, and, like most articles of the kind, costs five times as much bought in small quantities. From three tea-spoonfuls to half a wine-glass, proves a cathartic according to the constitution. It had better not be used for a year; for it improves by age. A tea-spoonful morning, noon, and evening, is good for those troubled with thread-worms. After this has been continued for some time, it is well likewise to take at bed-time, injections o fthree tea-spoonfuls of elixir, and the same quantity of lime water, in a gill of warm milk.

A tea-spoonful of elixir with an equal portion of red lavender is strengthening to weak stomachs. Red lavender simply dropped on sugar is comforting to the feeble and aged.

Sulphur.

Flour of sulphur is gently laxative, and promotes insensible perspiration. Principally used for cutaneous

disorders, and diseases of the blood. Dose from one
to three tea-spoonfuls, stirred in molasses or milk;
taken twice or three times a week. Often mixed with
an equal portion of supertartrite of potash, or with
magnesia. Sulphur transpires through the pores of the
skin ; the odor is usually perceived ; and it blackens
silver in the pocket. Sometimes used in rheumatism
and gout, asthmas, and chronic catarrhs. For the rheumatism it must be given in table-spoonful doses, and
the person remain in doors for a week, and keep warm.

Olive Oil, or Sweet Oil.

Nutritious and mildly laxative. Applicable to cases
of inward irritation, where the patient objects to more
disagreeable medicines. In large quantities, it mitigates
the effect of acrid *narcotic* poisons. Considered good
for worms. Recommended to pregnant women, internally and externally. In very common use to extract the heat from burns and scalds ; cotton being laid
over it. When pure it is devoid of smell.

Cajuput Oil.

Highly stimulating and penetrating, producing heat,
and sometimes profuse perspiration. Given for palsy,
chronic rheumatism, and spasmodic affections of the
stomach and bowels, not accompanied with inflammation. It has been much extolled in spasmodic cholera.
Dose from one to five drops on sugar, or with some
liquid. Mixed with an equal portion of olive oil, it is
a good liniment for gout and rheumatism. Its most remarkable effect is in curing the tooth-ache : from whatever cause the pain may arise, a few drops on cotton,
placed in the cavity of the tooth, or even around the
gums, are generally sure to give relief. It occasions
smart pain for an instant.

Turpentine.

Oil of turpentine irritates and inflames the skin. Used as a liniment in rheumatic and paralytic affections. In mild cases it should be diluted with olive oil ; and some constitutions cannot bear it even in this softened state. Mixed with some mild oil, and put into the ear on cotton, said to be good for deafness arising from a deficient or unhealthy secretion of wax. Much recommended for burns and scalds ; put on as soon as possible, on lint, or linen rags, being careful not to touch the sound flesh; removed as soon as the inflammation subsides.

Dr. Dewees says, he prescribed, for tape-worms, an ounce of spirits of turpentine mixed with an ounce of castor oil, to be taken once a week, for three weeks. The medicine operated powerfully, and had the desired effect. The patient had been an athletic man, and of course could bear larger doses than a feeble person. Tape-worms produce emaciation, paleness, and a gnawing sensation at the pit of the stomach, which nothing appeases but almost constant eating.

Spirits of turpentine is excellent to bathe chilblains. Mixed with equal portions of spirits of wine, and applied with a feather, it is said to be good for St. Anthony's fire. Care should be taken not to touch the eyes.

Gum Guaiacum.

A hot, acrid medicine, given in rheumatic and other pains, when unaccompanied by fever. An ounce may be dissolved in a pint of new rum ; or powdered and rubbed with an ounce of gum arabic, and put into a pint of water, sweetened. A tea-spoonful in a wine-glass of milk may be taken three times a day, to prevent rheumatism from striking to the stomach. Dropped on cotton, it relieves the tooth-ache.

It is diuretic ; and, when taken warm, produces perspiration ; for this purpose it is sometimes used to keep

9

out cutaneous eruptions, when not attended with inflammation. In large doses, it purges.

It is an ingredient in the following efficacious emmenagogue :—Red oxyde of iron, and pulverized rhubarb, each one ounce ; aloes, white canella, and gum Guaiacum, each half an ounce ; dissolved in three half pints of Holland gin, and well shaken. One tea-spoonful may be taken twice a day as a tonic, and occasionally a table-spoonful as a cathartic. At the return of every four weeks, soak the feet in warm water, take a rather larger dose than common, and be careful about exposure to cold.

Camphor.

A fragrant gum, that cannot be dissolved without alcohol, or expressed oil. A small bottle of it is usually kept in families. As much gum is put in as the rum will dissolve ; if particles remain floating in it, it may be occasionally filled up. The smell is good for nervous head-ache and faintness ; likewise comforting to bathe the hands, feet, and forehead, in cases of dry skin and nervous restlessness. It is a good anodyne wash for rheumatic and muscular pains. A small tea-spoonful of the tincture in a gill or more of water, is good for wind. Used in several spasmodic diseases.

It cannot safely be given in larger doses than half a drachm. The medium dose is from five to ten grains ; in extreme weakness, but one grain. Mixed with some fluid it is less apt to excite nausea than when taken in substance. A weak preparation, called water of camphor, is usually given in low fevers, nervous debility, &c. It is thus made :—Wet one scruple of camphor with ten drops of alcohol ; put to it half a scruple of magnesia ; add a pint of warm water gradually. Filter through paper. Some add half an ounce of sugar instead of magnesia. Two table-spoonfuls may be taken every hour or two.

The smell of the gum is said to relieve that unpleasant fulness of the nostrils, which attends commencing catarrh.

Cayenne.

A powerful rubefacient, that promptly stimulates the skin without blistering. Sprinkled on flannel wet with heated spirit, it is applied for violent pain in the bowels, and as a wash for rheumatism.

When people apply such hot external remedies for the rheumatism, it is well to take something two or three times a day, to prevent its striking to the heart, or stomach; guaiacum, an infusion of Cayenne, or of prickly-ash, are suitable. Internally, Cayenne is a very strong stimulant, producing a general glow. It is applicable to palsy and lethargic affections, and useful to correct flatulence in languid stomachs. In powder, the dose is from five to ten grains; most convenient made into a pill. To make the infusion, pour half a pint of boiling water upon two drachms of the powder, steep it an hour, and strain it; three or four tea-spoonfuls taken at once.

Cayenne may be made of the common red pepper, dried and powdered; but the process is troublesome to the eyes.

Opodeldoc, or Soap Liniment.

Shavings of hard soap, two ounces; camphor one ounce; very strong spirit one pint. Mix the soap with the spirit and keep it moderately warm till it is dissolved; then add the camphor, and shake it often. Some add half an ounce of the oil of rosemary, or a great spoonful of sweet oil. Excellent bath for swellings and rheumatic pains. Applied by a warm fire, and the limb covered with flannel.

Volatile Liniment.

Two thirds sweet oil, and one third hartshorn; shaken well, and corked very tight. Rubbed on stiff necks, rheumatic limbs, and to prevent sore throat.

Dr. Dean's Vegetable Rheumatic Pills.

Their reputation as a relief in cases of rheumatism is well founded. Directions accompany them.

Ginger.

Stimulant and carminative. Good for dyspepsia and flatulence. If taken in powder, from ten grains to a scruple is a dose. An infusion made by steeping half an ounce of the powder, or bruised root, in a pint of boiling water; quarter or half a gill may be taken. Applied outwardly it is rubefacient. The powder, when snuffed, excites violent sneezing. Often added to bitter and tonic medicines to give them a warming and cordial effect.

Cinnamon, Cloves, Carroway, &c.

Cinnamon is one of the pleasantest and most efficient of the aromatics. Carminative and astringent. Good for nausea and languid digestion. Of the powder, from ten grains to a scruple is a dose. Of the oil, one or two drops in some liquid.

Cloves are chewed as a stimulant for similar purposes; likewise for tooth-ache. Carroway, and fennel seed are often steeped for infants troubled with wind. All these articles, as well as orange-peal, are used to cover the taste of disagreeable medicines, and diminish their griping effect.

Liquorice.

A useful demulcent, much employed in various mixtures for coughs. A piece held in the mouth and slowly dissolved, is good for colds. The Italian is better than the Spanish.

Squills.

In small doses expectorant, and diuretic ; and if the patient is kept warm, produces profuse perspiration. One grain is given two or three times a day, and gradually increased till it occasions slight nausea, or evinces its action upon the kidney or lungs, by promoting the desired discharge. It is generally given to children in syrup, or honey. In substance it is usually swallowed as a pill. Where there is inflammation, squills should not be administered till it begins to subside. Large doses are emetic, and sometimes purgative ; from six to ten grains will commonly produce vomiting. In over-doses, it has produced fatal inflammation.

Balsam of Tolu.

A stimulant tonic, used as an expectorant in hard coughs, catarrh, and other pectoral complaints, not accompanied with active inflammation. Well mixed with gum arabic and loaf sugar, and afterward with water it makes an emulsion, of which a table-spoonful may be taken several times a day, with great benefit. The following PECTORAL SYRUP is very salutary for hard coughs, in the same doses :--Gum Arabic 2 ounces ; syrup of Tolu 1 ounce ; paregoric 2 drachms ; wine of ipecac half an ounce. The WHITE MIXTURE, for the same purpose, is made of lacc ammoniac five ounces and a half ; syrup of Tolu one ounce ; wine of ipecac half an ounce ; paregoric half an ounce.

Ipecacuanha.

A South American root, used as a mild, efficient emetic. It is suitable to all ages, and may be repeated with perfect safety. In asthma, whooping-cough, &c.,
9*

it is given to excite nausea ; in doses of two grains, repeated according to circumstances.   The same quantities are used to check hemorrhage.   One grain in flax-
seed tea is given as an expectorant, in catarrh and
other pulmonary complaints.   It promotes perspiration,
and is considered an appropriate emetic for fevers.
Twenty grains of the powder are usually given, stirred
in water, to a grown person ; if this does not induce
vomiting, it may be safely repeated at intervals of
twenty minutes.   Of the wine of ipecac, two table-
spoonfuls is a common emetic dose.   Mixed together,
in the proportion of twenty grains of the powder to an
ounce of the wine of ipecac, is the best form of taking
it, because it is at once thorough and safe.   This mixture is not recommended for children ; but a table-
spoonful, repeated every fifteen minutes till it operates
freely, is a salutary and sufficient emetic for grown
persons, on all common occasions.

Antimony.

A mineral preparation much used by physicians.
Emetic doses have very different effects on different
constitutions, and are not always safe.   This is a sufficient reason for not prescribing them in a book for
popular use.

As an *expectorant*, it is considered a specific in lung
fevers, and the first stages of severe colds accompanied
with inflammation.   For this purpose, half a tea-spoonful of wine of antimony is stirred in a tumbler of flax-
seed tea, and a draught taken frequently.   Care is
necessary about exposure to cold while the pores are
open.

Opium.

A powerful narcotic, to be used with very great caution.   In small quantities it quiets the nerves and induces drowsiness.   The medium dose for a grown person

is from one to two grains, but in some cases not more than one third or one fourth of a grain is administered. People who are so unwise as to use it frequently, become accustomed to considerable quantities ; but the effects are ruinous. This drug is obtained from the common poppy. The Asiatic mode is to make lengthwise incisions in the green seed-vessels, the moment the flowers fall ; a juice exudes, which is scraped off the next day when dry. This is opium. But a better mode is to cut off the stalk, about an inch below the seed vessel, as soon as the flowers begin to fall. Take off the milky juice that slowly exudes in drops, and put it upon an earthen plate to dry. Then cut the stalk about an inch lower, and proceed the same.

Laudanum.

This is tincture of opium ; made by steeping two ounces and a half of the powder in a quart of rectified spirits ; remain fourteen days, and be filtered through paper. Twenty-five drops are equal to one grain of opium ; considerably less will affect those unused to it ; fifteen drops would probably be the safest medium. When it acts as a vomit, check it with strong hot coffee, without sugar or milk ; a great-spoonful at first, and repeated till relief is obtained. Fifteen drops of laudanum with fifteen drops of essence of peppermint is recomended to prevent the repetition of convulsion fits, and is likewise good for cramp in the stomach.

For bleeding at the lungs, give ten drops of laudanum every fifteen minutes while bleeding ; and afterward every six hours till the vessel is healed, which is usually in about five days. Bathe the hands and feet with warm water, and rub them frequently. Give laxative injections. Keep the patient very calm and still, leaning backward.

Laudanum diluted with water is good to apply to fresh wounds. When long kept, it becomes thick and is much more powerful ; of course, doses must be diminished. Opium, in all its forms, has a constipating effect.

Paregoric.

This is a weaker form, called camphorated tincture of opium. A pleasant elixir, used to allay coughs, quiet nervous, wakeful people, &c. A grown person may take two tea-spoonfuls, or a table-spoonful. Consumptive patients generally require its frequent use; and in such cases it is more economical to prepare it at home, than to buy it in small quantities. It is made thus :---Opium, benzoic acid, and volatile oil of anniseed, each one drachm; camphor, two scruples; rectified spirits, one quart. Steeped ten days, and filtered through paper.

Citric Acid, and Tartaric Acid.

Half a tea-spoonful stirred in a gill of water is good for the head-ache, unless the pain proceeds from excess of acid in the stomach. Tartaric acid is the cheapest, and as good for common purposes.

The best substitute for lemon juice is crystalized citric acid, dissolved in water; about an ounce to a pint; with sugar, and one or two drops of oil of lemon. Lemon juice is much valued as a preventive and cure of scurvy. Ships destined to long voyages, should be supplied with the concentrated juice of lemons, or with the substitute just mentioned.

Soda Powders.

Cooling healthy drink in summer. Twenty-five grains of tartaric acid, and half a drachm of bi-carbonate of soda, in separate papers. The acid should be well dissolved in a wine-glass of water in one tumbler, and the soda in another. They effervesce when mingled. Most people think them more agreeable with syrup or sugar.

Rochelle Powders, or Seidlitz Powders.

Two drachms of the tartrate of potash and soda (sold under the name of Rochelle salts) and two scruples of bi-carbonate of soda, mixed together, and done up in white paper ; thirty-five grains of tartaric acid in blue paper. Dissolved separately. They effervesce when mixed. This is a gentle aperient, sometimes purgative. The excess of acid renders it more pleasant, without injuring its laxative quality.

Both these and soda powders might be bought cheap in considerable quantities, for family use ; experience would soon enable a person to measure the proportions with a tea-spoon, without the trouble of weighing.

Effervescing Draughts, or Neutral Mixture.

Quarter of a gill of water with fifteen grains of the carbonate of potash dissolved in it ; the same quantity of liquid composed of half lemon-juice and half water. If these do not effervesce when mixed, more lemon should be added. These draughts are repeated every two or three hours, to allay irritability, and produce perspiration in intermittent fevers.

Vinegar.

Refrigerant, diuretic, and antiseptic. Often added to drinks in putrid fevers and pestilential disorders. It has a good effect when there are white deposits in the urine, consisting of phosphate of lime, &c. A good wash for bruises and sprains. Diluted with water, best means of clearing the eyes from particles of lime. The smell is good for fainting, nausea, hysteria, &c. The hot steam, inhaled through the small end of a tunnel, is good for sore throat ; children should try it carefully at first, lest the throat be scalded. Poured into a hot shovel, or pan, it covers disagreeable smells in a room. Frequent washing in hot vinegar is recommended for ring-worms, and fellons.

Alum.

Powerfully astringent. A weak solution held in the mouth is excellent for canker. Fried and powdered, it is very good to sprinkle upon cankered mouths and proud-flesh. Alum is used to stop bleeding of various kinds, in the form of solution, wash, gargle, and a female injection ; the latter consists of alum and water, administered with the uterine syringe ; it is taken for the same purposes that alum-whey is drank, and is by many considered safer and better.

From five to twenty grains of alum are repeated every hour or two in cases of alarming hemorrhage. The dose should be small, except in very urgent cases.

Alum-whey is made by boiling two drachms of alum in a pint of new milk, and straining it. It is given in cases of excessive flowing owing to miscarriage, and other causes. A wine-glass full is repeated every hour or two in the course of the day ; stop giving it when it excites nausea. It should be remembered that astringents applied in this way are often extremely hazardous ; women have sometimes become permanently insane in consequence. Alum-whey is given only in urgent cases, where the continued difficulty produces faintness, pale lips &c., and threatens life. Two or three spoonfuls of clear rum poured down the throat occasions a revulsion, and stops the flowing of blood immediately ; its use requires the same caution as alum-whey.

Old port wine, and water with loaf sugar and nutmeg, is a useful astringent in such cases, but not powerful. The diet should consist of gruel, arrow-root, &c.

Peruvian Bark, or Cinchona.

A celebrated astringent tonic. Physicians recommend its early use, in divided doses, during the intermission of the paroxysms in fever and ague ; one drachm, more or less frequently, according to circumstances; in water, or some aromatic infusion. In low forms of disease, when inflammation has subsided, it is used as a tonic ; thus in the last stages of scarlet fever, measles, small pox, gangrenous erysipelas, and in all cases of convalescence where the system is exhausted by purulent discharges ; likewise for scrofula, hysteria, &c. ; in small doses, from ten to thirty grains, to begin with. When there are local irritations or inflammation, it should never be used in any form.

Two tea-spoonfuls, several times a day, are taken for the same purposes as alum-whey ; it is less powerful ; but it is well to remember the caution about checking too suddenly, except in emergencies.

This bark, and other astringent medicines, are used for fluor albus. To indulge much in bed, to keep late hours, to use stimulating drinks, or high-seasoned food, or drink immediately of tea and coffee, all tend to increase this weakness : the frequent use of the warm bath, or of foot-stoves, is likewise injurious. Thorough cleanliness cannot be too highly recommended both as a preventive and a remedy. Lukewarm water should be frequently applied, and warm suds often employed with a syringe, after the manner of female injections. A strengthening plaster on the lower part of the back is useful. Avoid long walks, or being much on the feet.

Assafœtida.

A drug of exceedingly disagreeable taste and smell. A powerful antispasmodic, much given in hysteria, and nervous debility, when not accompanied by inflammation. Taken as a pill, ten grains is the medium dose. One drachm of assafœtida in half a pint of pennyroyal water makes a white mixture, called milk of assafœtida, generally considered the best form for an antispasmodic ; one or two table-spoonfuls may be frequently repeated.

As an efficient expectorant assafœtida is given in whooping-cough, asthma, catarrh, and other pulmonary complaints, either in the form of pill, or an emulsion made by gradually adding and mixing two drachms of assafœtida with half a pint of water.

Lime Water.

Half a pound of lime in six quarts of water, well dissolved by frequent shaking; strinaed through paper, or thick cloth, and corked tight. It will keep a long time. The lime is better for being recently burnt. . It is used as a caustic wash for scald head, ulcerous eruptions, &c. Good for those troubled with an acid stomach, but when long continued weakens the powers of digestion. Half a gill or more may be drunk daily. Its acrid taste is best concealed by mixing with new milk.

Chloride of Lime.

This cheap article has wonderful power to resist putrefaction, and purify the air from bad odors. It is very useful to those who live in small rooms and dirty lanes. A table-spoonful stirred in a gill of water, should be put in a saucer or deep plate, and renewed daily. In warm weather, it is prudent to place it near coffins. A tea-spoonful stirred in water and placed in a night-vessel before it is used, will prevent disagreeable odors.

Sugar of Lead, or Acetate of Lead.

For small children one scruple of lead is dissolved in half a pint of soft water. For grown people, a drachm in a gill and a half of water is a strong solution; a gill of water added renders it a weak one. Used as a wash, or cloths wet with it, for inflamed eyes, piles, and virulent eruptions. Care must be taken that the bandages are not so wet as to have it enter the eyes. When applied to eruptions, a dose of salts should be taken occasionally, and snake-root be used to keep it from striking to the stomach. In cases of sudden eruptions, it is well to take advice concerning their nature ; for this application is sometimes dangerous.

Charcoal.

Remarkable for antiputrescent qualities. In dyspepsia attended with fetid breath, it has a purifying influence. It checks nausea and heart-burn, and has a salutary effect when the bowels are in a very restricted state.

Chewed slowly, it tends to preserve the teeth from decay. The charcoal of wood is commonly used ; but in diseases some prefer that of cocoa-nut, or bread. A tea-spoonful, or a table-spoonful, may be taken in syrup, milk, or water. Cork burned to charcoal, and a tea-spoonful of the powder mixed with loaf sugar and a few drops of essence of peppermint, is very efficacious in dysentery and cholera morbus.

Mrs. Kidder's Cordial.*

I mention this merely because I know it to be a very valuable family medicine, for various forms of diarrhea &c. It may be safely used for old people, or children. Directions accompany each bottle.

———

HERBS AND ROOTS.

Of annual plants, the leaves, stems, and blossoms are generally employed for medicinal purposes. They should be gathered in blossom, dried thoroughly, and kept in paper bags well preserved from the air. Herb tea should be made quite strong. An ounce of the plant steeped an hour or two in a pint of boiling water, is usually sufficient.

Of perennial plants, the roots are commonly used.

* Sold No. 9, Poplar Street, Boston.

They should be dug quite late in the autumn, or very early in the spring ; and, when dry, be kept carefully covered in bottles or jars.

The efficacy of all vegetable medicines is more or less diminished by time ; therefore it is well to have a fresh stock every year. When purchased, care should be taken to observe whether they are free from mould, and retain their taste and fragrance.

Herbs are prepared for use in the following ways :— Decoction, by boiling in water ; infusion, by steeping in boiling water ; powder, by bruising ; extract or essence, by distillation ; expressed juice, by squeezing ; tincture, by steeping in alcohol.

The habitual use of tinctures and essences is full of danger. Many an invalid has unconsciously formed intemperate habits by means of these seductive medicines.

Bitter herbs are generally tonic, and large doses are apt to induce vomiting ; it is therefore better to take them cold ; about a wine-glass full at once.

Aromatic stimulants are good for wind, nausea, nervous spasms, &c. Neither tonics or stimulants should he given where there are signs of fever.

Herbs to promote perspiration should be drunk hot, and the patient well covered in a warm bed. Half a pint or more may be taken. Vegetable diaphoretics commonly have more or less of a *heating* tendency ; therefore unsuited to fevers.

Diuretics should be taken in the day-time ; because external warmth stops their effect, and changes them to diaphoretics.

Astringents are employed as an antiseptic wash for ulcerated throats, sores, &c. They are given to allay the spitting of blood, and to check dysentery, *after the inflammation has subsided.*

Wormwood. (Artemisia Absinthium.)

An infusion of the leaves has great reputation as a tonic bitter for debilitated stomachs. A wine-glass full

is a common dose, taken early in the morning. It is
less likely to induce head-ache in nervous persons if
boiled, instead of steeped. A strong decoction is
good to cleanse ulcerated sores, &c. It is likewise a
very strengthening application for bruises and sprains ;
and the essence of wormwood in such cases operates
like a charm. The bruised green leaves are excellent
for fresh bruised wounds ; when the herb is dry, it
must be moistened with warm vinegar, or water, before
it is applied.

Frequent washing in a cold injusion of wormwood
and mustard seed is said to be good for numb and
trembling hands.

Chamomile. (*Anthemis Nobilis.*)

An infusion of the blossoms is a mild tonic, good
for enfeebled digestion and languid appetite. Recommended as an emmenagogue ; likewise given for flatulence, and spasmodic diseases. It is administered between the paroxysms of intermittent fever, when Peruvian bark is considered too powerful. A luke-warm
infusion is often taken to assist the operation of *vegetable* emetics. May weed, (*Anthemis Cotula*,) is called
wild chamomile, because it resembles this plant in appearance and medicinal qualities.

Sage. (*Salviæ Officinalis.*)

Slightly tonic and astringent. A strong infusion of
the plant relieves the head-ache, and is much used for
that which accompanies measles and canker-rash. The
exhausting night-sweats attending hectic fevers have
sometimes been cured by fasting morning and night,
and drinking cold sage-tea constantly and freely. It
checks nausea, invigorates a feeble appetite, and in small
quantities is good for weak and windy stomachs. Mixed with honey and vinegar it is a good gargle for sore
throats. A weak infusion, with a little lemon juice and

sugar, is safe and pleasant drink in fevers. The powdered leaves taken freely in molasses are much recommended for worms.

Black Oak. (*Quercus Tinctoria.*)

The bark is astringent and somewhat tonic. Given with advantage in intermittent fevers, and permanent diarrhea. A decoction is much recommended as a bath for children, when a combined tonic and astringent is desired, and the stomach does not receive medicines kindly. It has been used in this way for scrofula, chronic diarrhea, and the latter stages of cholera infantum.

Wild Cherry Tree. (*Prunus Virginiana.*)

The bitter aromatic bark is one of the most valuable of native remedies. It is a tonic, at the same time that it calms irritation and nervous excitability ; of course, it is very useful where debility is accompanied with inflammation. Often used in the hectic fever of scrofula and consumption, and applied to many cases of dyspepsia. Half an ounce of the bruised bark steeped twenty-four hours in a pint of cold water. Half a gill drunk three or four times a day, or oftener. Sometimes the powder is used, in doses of two or three teaspoonfuls. The bark of the root is more powerful than that of the trunk. A decoction is good to wash ill-conditioned ulcers.

Thorough-wort; Thorough-wax; Cross-wort; Bone-set; (*Eupatorium Perfoliatum.*)

A cold infusion of the flowers is by many preferred to chamomile, as a tonic stimulant. Some prefer to take one or two tea-spoonfuls of the leaves and flowers in powder, or rolled into pills. A warm infusion assists the operation of emetics. A considerable quantity taken strong, without sweetening, of itself induces vomiting and perspiration. Even a cold infusion is diaphoretic, and therefore given to promote moisture in fevers. An ounce of the plant boiled in a quart of water till reduced to a pint, sweetened with half a gill of W. I. molasses, forms a mild cathartic that corrects bile, without weakening the system. A wine-glass may be taken.

Buck Bean; Marsh Trefoil. (*Menyanthes Trifoliata.*)

Root used either in powder or decoction. Resembles thorough-wort in its effects. A tonic in small doses ; but two or three gills of the strong warm decoction produce vomiting, purging, and perspiration.

Butternut Tree. (*Juglans Cinerea.*)

The inner bark of the tree, and especially of the root, is a very mild and efficacious laxative. It is much employed in dysentery ; and when the system is habitually restricted, it is better than more stimulating physic. Some drink a decoction, others make it into pills. Boil it with water enough to cover it. Renew the water as it boils away, for an hour or two. Strain it, and simmer it down, till it becomes thick as molasses. Be careful not to burn it. When cool, make it into common-sized pills ; of which two, three, or more, may be taken, according to circumstances. People troubled with weak or windy stomachs, sometimes shake in a little cinnamon, or pepper, before it is made into pills. An extract of butternut is sold, of which a tea-spoonful operates gently, and twice as much actively.

May Apple ; Wild Lemon. (*Podophyllum Peltatum.*)

A decoction of the root is a sure and active cathartic. Dr. Bigelow says, " We have hardly any native plant which answers better the common purposes of

10*

jalap, aloes, and rhubarb, and which is more safe and mild in its operation." Some consider it a good medicine for dropsy ; and it has been used in the southern states for curing intermittent fever. The Shakers prepare an extract of podophyllum much esteemed as a mild cathartic. A tea-spoonful of the powder usually operates with efficacy, without pain or inconvenience.

American Senna; Wild Senna. (*Cassia Marylandica.*)

The leaves and stems, in strong infusion or decoction, are a very good substitute for the imported senna. It is such a mild physic, that one third more of it is required.

Double Tanzy. (*Tanacetun Crispum*) *Single Tanzy.* (*Tanacetum Vulgare.*)

Very much recommended as an emmenagogue. The oil is so powerful that a few drops destroy life immediately ; and the essence should not be taken without medical advice. A strong decoction, or infusion, of the herb is in common use. Some prefer a syrup, made thus :—Put into the oven a jar of tanzy just covered with water ; bake it an hour or two ; add half a pint of gin to the strained liquor ; sweeten it, and cork it in bottles. Half a wine glass may be taken two or three times a day.

Wild Carrot. (*Daucus Carota.*)

An ounce and a half of the seed steeped in a pint of boiling water is a very efficacious emmenagogue, and a diuretic used in cases of dropsy, stranguary, &c. The seed of the common cultivated carrot answers a similar purpose ; and a marmalade of the roots is recommended for sea-scurvy, on account of their antiseptic qualities. A strong tea made of them is said to have relieved people afflicted with tape-worms.

Penny Royal. (Hedeoma Pulegiodes.)

An aromatic ; good for flatulence, and checks sickness at the stomach. Half a pint of the strong infusion of the herb, taken hot when going to bed, is much used as an emmenagogue in common cases ; and is likewise excellent to produce perspiration, when people have taken cold, with feverish symptoms.

Calamint. (Melissa Nepeta.) Horsemint. (Mentha Borealis.)

These resemble penny royal, in fragrance, taste, and qualities.

Peppermint. (Mentha Piperita.)

In more general use than the other mints, for wind, spasmodic pains, nausea, &c.; likewise to cover the taste of disagreeable medicines, and diminish their griping effects. The fresh herb bruised and applied to the pit of the stomach often allays sickness, and is especially useful in the cholera of children. Of the strong infusion, a gill or two may be drunk occasionally. Of the essence, fifteen or twenty drops in a little hot water sweetened. Of the oil, two or three drops. The essence, applied two or three times, is sure to scatter blisters forming on the lips, if it be done as soon as their approach is suspected.

Spearmint. (Mentha Viridis.)

Qualities similar to peppermint, but less bracing.

Catmint ; Catnep. (Nepeta Cataria.)

A mild aromatic, that tends to promote perspiration, and is often mixed with penny royal for that purpose.

The infusion, sweetened with molasses is a common remedy for children troubled with wind-colic. It is good for the mother to drink, while nursing.

Sweet-scented Golden Rod. (Solidago Odora.)

The oil obtained from the leaves is a gentle stimulant, tending to produce perspiration ; possessing the qualities of peppermint, and other aromatics. From its spicy flavor, much used to cover the taste of laudanum and other disagreeable medicines, when rejected by the stomach.

Chequer Berry ; Box Berry ; Mountain Tea. (Gaultheria Procumbens.)

In much estimation as a warm aromatic stimulant. The oil, like that of peppermint, diminishes the sensibility of the nerve, when repeatedly applied to a decayed tooth. A strong infusion of the leaves is recommended as an emmenagogue, in cases attended with debility. A tea-spoonful of the essence, in a tumbler of sweetened water, is a pleasant and refreshing drink.

Petty Morel; Spikenard ; Life of Man. (Aralia Racemosa.)

A much-esteemed aromatic. An infusion of the berries is recommended for rheumatism. A decoction of the root is good for flatulence, and considered very salutary for humors. Mixed with dandelions, it forms a drink very beneficial for weakly people troubled with wind.

Wild Sarsaparilla. (Aralia Nudicaulis.)

A strong decoction of the roots is recommended for scrofula and other humors. A gill may be taken frequently. The Spanish Sarsaparilla, if new and well preserved, is considered more efficacious than our native plant.

Winter Evergreen; Pipsissiwa; Rheumatism Weed. (Pyrola Umbellata.)

This trailing plant has high reputation. It acts as a tonic in promoting strength and appetite. As a diuretic, it is much praised in cases of stranguary, dropsy, and various disorders of the kidneys. For humors, ulcers, and tumors, it is excellent ; applied both externally and internally. Drank freely and perseveringly, it is said to have cured cancers. The wash is a stimulant, like bitter sweet. A strong decoction, or infusion, is made of the leaves and stems ; sweetened with molasses, or syrup. Drank very often, and in any quantities. It is well to discontinue it occasionally, and renew it, lest the system become too much accustomed to it. It has been celebrated in cases of chronic rheumatism.

Bitter Sweet; Woody Nightshade; Nature's Wax Work. (Solanum Dulcamara.)

A decoction of the leaves and twigs is highly recommended for cancers, ring-worms, itch, and other cutaneous eruptions. Half a gill may be taken morning, noon, and night, and increased to a pint a day according to its effects. In delicate constitutions it sometimes occasions giddiness and vomiting. Such persons should try a quarter of a gill at first. The addition of cinnamon, or some aromatic, renders it less liable to offend the stomach. The good effects are seldom perceived under eight or ten days. Humors are often bathed with it, while it is taken internally ; but when the surface is inflamed, this, and other external stimulants, are injurious.

Curled Dock; Wild Rhubarb. (Rumex Crispus.)

The root is tonic and astringent, and at the same time laxative, like rhubarb. An ounce boiled in a pint of water ; half a gill taken at once, as the stomach can bear it. Much used in decoction, for humors ; and employed as a bath for the same purpose. The leaves boiled for greens are slightly laxative, and good for scorbutic disorders.

Broad-leaved Dock ; Butter Dock. (Rumex Obtusifolius.)

The root has the same peculiar medicinal qualities as the curled species. Much recommended prepared as ointment for cutaneous eruptions.

Dandelion. (Leontodon Taraxacum.)

Slightly tonic, diuretic, and aperient. The leaves eaten as greens are excellent for the blood. The milky juice is good for stranguary, dropsy, and inflammation of the liver ; two or three table-spoonfuls several times a day. A strong decoction of the roots and leaves is good for the same purpose ; a gill may be drunk requently.

Bear Berry ; Wild Cranberry ; Mountain Cranberry. (Arbutus Uva Ursi.)

Astringent and diuretic. Very highly recommended for dropsy, paroxysms brought on by gravelly concretions, and other diseases of the kidneys. Of the powdered leaves from five to ten or more grains is a dose. A decoction is made by boiling an ounce of the plant ten minutes in a pint of water. A gill may be taken every hour.

Common Juniper. (*Juniperus Communis.*)

On account of their diuretic effects, a decoction of the bruised berries is much used in stranguary, dropsy, &c. It is said to be good for old people with weak stomachs. European Juniper is stronger than American, if it retains the aromatic taste ; but the virtue is often extracted before it is sold.

Red Cedar ; American Savin. (*Juniperus Virginiana.*)

A salve resembling the savin cerate is made of it. A decoction of the bruised leaves is taken for rheumatism, as a warm stimulant, producing perspiration.

Prickly Ash. (*Xanthoxylum Fraxineum.*)

Very highly recommended for chronic rheumatism. Effects similar to gum guaiacum. A decoction is made with an ounce of the bark boiled in a quart of water ; a pint may be taken in the course of the day. Sometimes given powdered ; about a tea-spoonful.

Sassafras Tree. (*Laurus Sassafras.*)

Valued as a warm stimulant and antispasmodic, producing perspiration. The oil obtained from the bark is preferred to a decoction, because the virtues of the plant partially evaporate by boiling. A few drops should be taken, mixed with sweetened water or syrup. The bark and young twigs abound with mild, delicate mucilage, much used in decoction as a wash for inflamed eyes ; likewise very soothing drink for catarrh, gravelly affections, and inflamed state of the bowels. Mixed with pumpkin-seed it makes an excellent tea for stranguary.

White Pine Tree. (*Pinus Strobus.*)

Frequent morning walks in pine woods are very in-
vigorating, particularly for consumptive people.   It is
even deemed healthy to have these trees in the vicinity
of dwellings.   The bark of the twigs, and young
trees, is very mucilaginous.   A decoction of it, when
dried, is a gentle and soothing laxative.   In its green
state it cannot be too highly praised as a strengthening
wash for weak joints, and healing and cleansing to inflamed wounds and sores.   The gum taken as pills is
very physical.

Hemlock Spruce Tree.   (*Pinus Canadensis.*)

The astringent bark, (used by tanners,) powdered
and sifted through muslin, dries the surface of the skin,
when chafed behind the ears, &c.   A decoction of the
twigs and leaves much recommended as a sedative
bath, in spotted or other malignant fevers.   For rheumatic pain in the bones, it is good to soak the feet in
very warm water, with hemlock branches steeped in it.
Keep covered with blankets, and get into a hot bed.
The pitch is used as a strengthening plaster.

Pitch Pine Tree.   (*Pinus Rigida.*)

Boil the knots till the pitch rises to the surface.
Spread on leather, it is a very strengthening plaster
for weak backs.   Many prefer it to all other similar
applications.   A little nutmeg grated on the surface is
an improvement.

Spruce Fir Tree.   (*Pinus Abies.*)

The exuding gum, boiled and strained, forms a plaster,
called Burgundy pitch, in very common use for weak
backs, pain in the side, &c.

Fir Balsam Tree. (Pinus Balsamea.)

The exuding balsam is called resin of Canada.
Rubbed up with gum arabic, or sugar, and then dissolved in water, a few tea-spoonfuls may be taken as
the system can bear it. It is laxative and diuretic ;
strengthening to the nervous system, and good for
chronic coughs not accompanied with inflammation.

Balm of Gilead Tree. (Populus Candicans.)

The leaf-buds are very resinous and fragrant. They
should be gathered when they are well swelled and just
ready to expand. They remain thus but two or three
days. Bottled in rum, they form a most excellent healing liniment for fresh cuts and wounds.

Hardhack. (Spiræa Tomentosa.)

Very astringent ; but less apt to disagree with the
stomach than most herbs of its kind. Used in advanced
stages of diarrhea and cholera infantum, when there are
no remaining signs of inflammation. Used as a tonic,
in cases of debility. A decoction of leaves and flowers ;
dose about half a gill. Mixed with thorough-wort, in
equal portions, it is recommended for chronic weakness
of the bowels.

Common Cranesbill ; Spotted Geranium. (Geranium Maculatum.)

A strong astringent; used in the same cases, and
with the same precautions as hardhack. It is often
boiled in milk for children. It has no unpleasant taste
or smell. The root is generally used ; either in decoction, or in powdered doses of a tea-spoonful or more,
for grown persons.

11

Tall Blackberry.   (*Rubus Villosus.*).

Decidedly astringent.   A tea made of the roots and leaves, and a syrup made of the berries, are both in common use to check a relaxed state of the bowels. It should never be used in the first stages, or while there are any feverish symptoms.

Low, Running Blackberry ;   Dewberry.   (*Rubus Procumbens.*)

Properties similar to the high blackberry.   Tea made of the leaves much used as an astringent wash, when the mouth is hot and sore, in fevers.

Marsh Rosemary.   (*Statice Caroliniana.*)

The root is astringent as galls.   In dysentery, continuing from weakness, after inflammation has subsided, it has proved efficacious when other tonics and astringents have been tried in vain.   For ulcers and sore mouths it is considered a much better wash than goldthread, with which it is often combined.   Internally and externally it has been very successful in cases of malignant sore throat.   A cold infusion is preferred, because some of the virtue evaporates by heat.   Steep from twelve to twenty-four hours.

Gold Thread.   (*Coptis Trifolia.*)

A strong decoction of the roots recommended as a tonic for indigestion.   In very common use as a wash for ulcerated and sore mouths.   Infants have it applied with a soft linen swab, often during the day.   Dr. Bigelow thinks its reputation unmerited in such cases, because it is simply a bitter, without astringency.

Sumach ; often called Shoemake. (Rhus Glabrum.)

The berries are astringent and refrigerant. An infusion of them is a pleasant drink in feverish complaints, and a good gargle for inflamed aud ulcerated throats : likewise given to check the spitting of blood.

Virginia Snake-Root. (Aristolochia Serpentaria.)

The roots are tonic and antispasmodic. Half an ounce may be well steeped in a pint of boiling water, and half a wine-glass full taken repeatedly, according to circumstances. It checks vomiting, and tranquillizes the stomach, particularly in bilious cases. It is very good to allay the delirium, watchfulness, &c. that often attend febrile debility ; but ought not to be used when the pulse is rapid. It is a popular diaphoretic to keep out measles, rash, and other eruptions ; but physicians consider it too stimulating, when there are signs of inflammation.

Saffron. (Crocus Sativus.)

An infusion of the flowers is stimulant, antispasmodic, and tends to produce sleep. Mixed with snake-root it is given to keep out measles, and prevent eruptions from striking to the stomach, when outward applications are made ; but some physicians doubt its efficacy in such cases. Large doses produce head-ache, stupor, and other disagreeable effects. It has been recommended as an emmenagogue.

Balm. (Melissa Officinalis.)

An infusion of the herb is a cooling drink in fevers. When taken warm, it aids medicines given for perspiration.

Motherwort. (Leonurus Cardiaca.)

Very quieting in nervous, hysterical complaints, and strengthening to weak stomachs. Half a pint of the strong, warm infusion will often induce refreshing sleep, when it cannot be obtained by other means. Drank plentifully and constantly, it is one of the very best regulators during that critical change in the constitutions of women approaching fifty years of age. Tonics and stimulants, though supported by popular opinion, are injurious at this time. Food and drink should be very simple and unexciting, and taken cool or cold. Full-blooded people should keep the system low by the occasional use of rhubarb or salts. Sleep on a mattrass, and admit the cool air freely. Avoid cold, damp places and violent exercise. If the feet are cold bathe them in warm water with three or four table-spoon-fuls of mustard powder in it ; rub them till they glow, and get into a warm bed. If troubled with excessive flowing, keep quiet as possible. Severe pain may be relieved by taking one grain of opium every six hours. Wear flannel next the skin, and be sure to keep the feet warm.

Skunk Cabbage ; Linn.   (*Ictodes Fœtidus.*)

The root and the seed are both used for anodyne qualities. For asthma, or nervous spasms, a tea-spoon-ful of the powdered root may be given in molasses, or syrup, and repeated at intervals till the patient is quieted. Twice that quantity each morning is said to be good for dropsy, rheumatism, and even epilepsy. A syrup made of the root has afforded great relief in asthma, chronic cough, and catarrh. The fresh root is sometimes steeped in cold water. Its qualities escape so easily, by heat or air, that it should be dried in thick slices, and not powdered till used. In delicate constitutions, over-doses sometimes occasion vomiting and vertigo.

The dangerous plant called poke *root*, or American Hellebore, grows in the same places, and closely re-sembles it in early spring. But skunk cabbage has a larger root, and every part, when broken, emits the disagreeable smell, from which it takes its name. It always remains a mere tuft of large leaves, like a cabbage ; while, as the season advances, the poke root sends up a very tall stalk.

Lettuce.

Water distilled from it is a mild sedative, without the constipating effects of opium. Grown people may take from half a gill to a gill. A tea made of the leaves, or milk squeezed from the plant, is a gentle opiate, to check chronic dysentery, allay coughs, and soothe nervous irritation.

Hop Vine. (*Humulus Lupulus.*)

A decoction of half an ounce of the blossoms in a pint of boiling water is a useful tonic. On account of its anodyne qualities, it is sometimes taken to procure sleep. Hop beer invigorates the stomach, when oppressed with dyspepsia, or feelings of lassitude in the spring. A bag filled with hops and wet with hot rum, or vinegar, is a quieting application for pain in the bowels, cramp in the stomach, ague in the face, &c. They are often moistened with spirit, so as to prevent a rustling noise, and then made into pillows for nervous and wakeful people. In poultices and fomentations they are used to soothe painful swellings, &c. The very young shoots eaten as asparagus, are reckoned healthy.

Apple of Peru; Thorn Apple ; Devil's Apple; Jamestown Weed. (*Datura Stramonium.*)

This plant when swallowed is a narcotic poison. The leaves, prepared like tobacco, and smoked, have given great relief in cases of pure spasmodic asthma. Applied to the part affected, or to the feet, they have been efficacious in removing spasms.

11*

Low Mallows. (Malva Rotundifolia.)

An infusion of the plant sweetened with W. I.
molasses is gently laxative. Very smooth and soothing
medicine for piles, dysentery, and inflammation of the
bowels.

Succory. (Cichorium Intybus.)

The same properties as low mallows. Consumptive
people will do well to use it freely.

Elder Bush. (Sambucus Canadensis.)

Tea made of the blossoms, sweetened with W. I.
molasses, or a syrup made of the berries, is safe and
gentle physic for small children. A few tea-spoonfuls
may be repeated according to circumstances. The
young leaf-buds are too strongly purgative for little
children.

Slippery Elm ; Red Elm. (Ulmus Fulva.)

A decoction of the bark drank plentifully, is an excellent demulcent in lung fevers, and much recommended for piles, dysentery, and consumption. A healing
wash for chilblains, eruptions, &c.

Elecampane. (Inula Helenium.)

Gently stimulant, tonic, diaphoretic, diuretic expectorant, and emmenagogue. Much used in chronic diseases
of the lungs and chest, attended with general debility.
Some take a tea-spoonful of the powdered root every
few hours ; others drink half a gill of the strong decoction frequently. A syrup is made by slicing the fresh
roots, covering them with sugar, and baking them an
hour or two.

White Horehound. (*Marrubium Vulgare.*)

A strong infusion of the herb sweetened with honey or W. I. molasses, is gently aperient, and promotes expectoration. Highly recommended for coughs and diseases of the lungs. Plentiful draughts of the warm infusion induce vomiting. A few tea-spoonfuls should be taken frequently, when cool.

Hyssop. (*Hyssopus Officinalis.*)

The bruised leaves are said to mitigate the pain of bruises and heal them without a scar. An infusion stimulates gently, and helps expectoration. Good for asthma, chronic catarrh, coughs, &c. especially in old, debilitated people. Elecampane, hyssop and horehound steeped together, and taken with warm flax-seed tea, when going to bed, is much praised as a cure for colds.

Colt's Foot; Wild Ginger; Canada Snake-root. (*Asarum Canadense.*)

The herb steeped in milk promotes perspiration, and is recommended for diseases of the lungs. It is thought the spicy root might be a substitute for ginger.

Silk Weed; Milk Weed. (*Asclepias Syriaca.*)

A strong infusion of the root has anodyne qualities. Good for the same diseases as hyssop.

Butterfly Weed; Pleurisy Root; Archangel. (*Aselepias Tuberosa.*)

A strong decoction of the root, taken several times a day is highly recommended by physicians for pulmo-nary consumption, pleurisy, catarrh, and various diseases of the lungs. It produces expectoration, relieves the difficulty of breathing, and throws the patient into a gentle perspiration, without the heating tendency of some vegetable medicines. Large doses are somewhat cathartic.

Marsh Mallows. (*Althea Officinalis.*)

The leaves and root both used to form a soothing drink for irritating coughs, catarrhal affections, an emollient gargle for sore throat, &c.

Ginseng. (*Panax Quinquefolium.*)

The root taken in decoction, or chewed, for the same purposes as liquorice.

Iceland Moss. (*Cetraria Islandica.*)

An ounce steeped in a pint of boiling water makes a drink demulcent, nutritious and tonic. Much recommended in chronic catarrhs, pulmonary complaints, and weakness occasioned by dysentery, or the copious discharge of external ulcers. Sometimes boiled into a jelly, strained and seasoned with lemon-juice and sugar.

Garlick. (*Allium Sativum.*)

A general stimulant that quickens circulation and excites the nervous system. When the patient is kept warm, its effects are diaphoretic. Taken cool, it is used as a diuretic, for dropsies and calculous disorders. As an expectorant, it is given in chronic catarrh, humoral asthma, whooping-cough, and other pectoral affections, after inflammation has subsided. In moderate quantities, it is good for flatulence and enfeebled digestion. Recommended for worms. The bulbs may be swallowed in slices, in pills, or made into a syrup taken in milk. A grown person may take half a clove, or a whole one, several times a day. Of the juice, about a tea-spoonful may be taken at once. It renders the breath extremely offensive. Large doses, especially in excited states of the system, are apt to occasion irritation, flatulence, and fever. Bruised and applied to the feet, it is good for disorders of the head, quiets restlessness, and produces sleep. The bruised root steeped in spirit, or the juice mixed with oil, is used as a wash in infantile convulsions, and other spasmodic disorders of children. A single clove, or a few drops of the juice on cotton, introduced into the ear, has proved highly efficacious in some cases of deafness.

Horse Radish. (*Cochlearia Armoracia.*)

The root promotes appetite and digestion. As an active stimulant, it is used both externally and internally for palsy and chronic rheumatism. As a diuretic, it is employed in dropsical disorders, particularly when the digestive powers are weak. Highly esteemed in scorbutic affections. Half a drachm or more may be taken, grated or sliced. A syrup made of it is good for a hoarse cold. Boiled in milk, it is said to be a good wash to remove tan and freckles. The leaves are a good application for rheumatic pains. They often relieve the tooth-ache, but if kept on the face too long will produce a blister. Bound on the feet, they are excellent for the head-ache and for colds attended with feverish symptoms. The stems should be cut out, they should be slowly wilted before the fire, or dipped in hot vinegar, clapped in the hands till they become soft, and then applied warm.

Burdock. (*Arctium Lappa.*)

These leaves have a quieting effect, and promote perspiration. They are soothing to inflamed surfaces, and are good to bind on the feet for nervous head-ache, burning in the feet, &c. A thick bat of them, applied very warm, relieves the pain in the bowels, that attends

dysentery and diarrhea. They should be prepared the
same as horse-radish, only no vinegar must be used.
A decoction of the root is aperient, diuretic, and
sudorific ; good for humors, gout, rheumatism, &c.
Tea made of the seed is good for stranguary.

Mullein. (*Verbascum Thapsus.*)

The leaves wilted in warm milk are applied for sore
throat ; and mixed with catmint are soothing to inflamed surfaces. In the latter case they should be renewed before they become dry. They should be gathered
from young plants, before the stalk runs up. An infusion of the flowers is given in mild catarrhs, and a
decoction of the leaves as an anodyne for diarrhea.

Plantain. (*Plantago Major.*)

The bruised leaves are a cooling application for inflamed sores, stings of insects, &c., and an ingredient
in soothing ointments. They are sometimes moistened
with warm milk. The expressed juice swallowed is
said to be good for the bite of venomous insects and
reptiles. Toads resort to it when bitten by spiders.
A slave in Carolina is said to have received his freedom
for curing the bite of a rattle-snake with the juice of
plantain and horehound, obtained from the bruised
roots and leaves. A table-spoonful poured down the
throat every hour, and tobacco moistened with rum applied to the wound.

Common Mustard. (*Sinapis Nigra.*)

The seed swallowed whole are a stimulating laxative
much recommended for dyspepsia. A table-spoonful
once or twice a day, soon after meals ; they may be
taken in molasses, or previously softened in hot water.
For rheumatism and palsy, they are taken every few
hours. White mustard is the kind generally preferred.

Two or three tea-spoonfuls of common powdered mustard is a rapid emetic, and is often used to hasten the operation of other emetics. It is thought well suited to cases of great torpor of stomach ; especially that produced by narcotic poisons. Native mustard is stronger than imported, and there is less liability to deception.

A Diet Drink, for Humors.

Burdock root ; curled dock root ; sarsaparilla root ; petty morel root. Leaves of the winter evergreen, or pipsissiwa ; bitter-sweet; chequer berry ; sprigs of sweet fern, unless the state of the system renders its astringent qualities undesirable. Boil the ingredients about an hour and a half. Strain it, and add a pint of W. I. molasses to a pailful, while hot. When blood-warm put a gill of lively yeast to a pailful. Let it remain in a jar or cask, till the froth on the top subsides to the thickness of a wafer. Then cork it tight in bottles.

POULTICES.

Whenever bark, leaves, blossoms, or seed, are mentioned in the following pages, as forming a poultice, it is meant that they are stewed in water, or milk, and thickened with crumbs of bread, or rye, or Indian meal. When wanted for soothing purposes, milk is better than water.

Poultices should generally be applied lukewarm, as soft as they will cohere together. They are usually changed every two or three hours; but in common cases, there is no need of rising in the night to attend to it. When there is great pain, they should be renewed more frequently.

Where mortification is apprehended, they should be changed often ; sometimes every fifteen or twenty minutes, night and day.   The approach of mortification is indicated by the formation of blisters filling with *blood* ; and its progress by the increasing blackness of surrounding parts.

The surface of poultices should always be soft and smooth ; therefore the presence of stems, hard veins, &c. ought to be avoided.   A fresh supply should be made often, in small quantities.

When applied to inflamed surfaces, sweet oil, linseed oil, or lard, spread upon the surface renders them more soothing, and prevents their adhering to the skin.   *The grease used for this purpose should always be very fresh and sweet.*

Biscuit Poultice is made by thickening boiling milk with powdered cracker, or crumbs of bread.   Much used as an emollient and suppurative, for felons, whitlows, inflamed sores, &c.   Oatmeal prepared in the same way is very emollient.

Flax-Seed, either whole or powdered, stirred plentifully into biscuit poultice, render it more soothing to inflamed surfaces, and promote suppuration.

Sumach.   The inner bark powdered, or scraped, and stewed soft, forms an excellent emollient poultice. If there is matter, it will bring it to a head ; if not, it will allay the swelling.

Low Mallows.   The fresh leaves form a soothing, suppurative poultice.

Slippery Elm.   The bark powdered, or finely shred, forms a very emollient application.

Marsh Mallows.   The roots make a very soothing poultice.

Hops,   prepared as a poultice, are very quieting.

Poppy blossoms are very quieting to rheumatic pains

in the head, burning wounds, &c. In case of great irritation, a soft linen rag dipped in very sweet oil, or soothing ointment, may be placed between the poultice and the wound.

Lettuce. The freshly gathered leaves have similar effects, but less in degree.

White Garden Lily. The scaly bulk forms a comforting suppurative poultice.

Skunk Cabbage. The sliced roots are made into a quieting poultice to relieve ague in the breast.

Figs, merely toasted, or boiled, and split open, are a good suppurative for parts where common poultices would be retained with difficulty ; such as gum-biles, &c.

White Beans merely stewed soft, and put on in thin muslin bags, are excellent to take down swellings.

Wheat Bran stirred in cold vinegar, and boiled till it becomes salvy, is a very quick cure for sprains. Rye bran will answer.

Yellow Water Lily, or *Skunk Lily.* (*Nuphar Advena.*) A poultice of the roots is very powerful in drawing tumors to a head. Much used for broken breasts.

White Pond Lily. (*Nymphea Odorata.*) A poultice of the sliced roots has astringent properties, similar to alum-curds. It has sometimes been very injudiciously employed when it was desirable to bring swellings to a head.

Alum-Curds are formed by stirring a tea-spoonful of pulverized alum into half a pint of warm milk. They are applied as an astringent to arrest mortification ; and are good to soothe proud flesh, and disperse the humors gathering round inflamed wounds. Renewed as soon as dry.

Vinegar Curds. Made in the same way, with vinegar instead of alum. They cool inflammation.

12

Alum Poultice. Stir the whites of two eggs briskly with a lump of alum till they coagulate. A good application for inflamed eyes, placed on the closed lids at night.

Rotten Apple. merely split open and placed on the lids, is very cooling to inflamed eyes. It retains its moisture much better than alum or vinegar-curds.

Roasted Apple is likewise a good application.

Indian Meal stirred into hot vinegar, and applied very warm, gives relief when there is violent pain in the bowels.

Carrots, merely boiled and mashed, are a emollient application for ulcers, &c. Scraped fresh, they are considered good for cancerous ulcers, the fetor of which they are supposed to correct. Boiled turnips and potatoes are used for emollient poultices.

Elder Blossoms are made into a poultice to prevent the approach of mortification.

Black Oak bark, powdered, or scraped very fine, forms a good astringent poultice for gangrene and mortification.

Charcoal, pulverized and plentifully stirred into biscuit-poultice arrests mortification, and is good for gangrene, ill-conditioned ulcers, &c.

Yeast Poultice is made by stirring a pound of wheat-flour into half a pint of lively yeast. Expose it to a gentle heat till it begins to ferment. A cleansing application for foul ulcers, &c.; and often used when alum-curds do not arrest the progress of mortification.

Horse Manure simmered in urine, and applied warm every fifteen or twenty minutes, is very powerful and efficacious, even in advanced stages of mortification. The natural color of the flesh will gradually return, and the mortified portions separate.

Cranberries stewed, applied as a poultice frequently and perseveringly, are recommended by Indian doctors as a cure for cancer.

Lady's Delight, sometimes called pansy, forget-me-not, *viola tri-color*, &c. A poultice of the blossoms said to cure the crusta lactea ; though for the first week it makes the disorder appear worse instead of better. A decoction of the plant is drunk occasionally.

Winter Evergreen, or *Pipsissina.* Tumors of long standing, have disappeared from the use of this stimulating poultice, renewed several times a day.

Ginger plentifully stirred in biscuit-poultice is applied to the face to relieve the tooth-ache.

Mustard Seed stirred into rye or Indian meal poultice, made with boiling water. They are applied to the soles of the feet, or the ancles, when people have a heavy cold, pain in the bones, &c. They frequently relieve violent tooth-ache ; but a thin rag had better be placed between them and the cheek, to avoid a blister. When the face is thoroughly hot, they can be removed, and renewed, if necessary.

If powdered mustard be spread on the surface of a rye poultice, it will be more likely to draw a blister. Such an application to the pit of the stomach soon checks vomiting and nausea, and may be removed before it blisters.

A tea-spoonful of powdered mustard, well mixed with a tea-spoonful of cold water, and spread about the thickness of a wafer on strong brown paper, is an excellent application for acute rheumatism, severe pain in the side, cramp in the stomach, &c. Applied to the chest, it is a valuable remedy when there is a heavy cold on the lungs, and the person is obliged to go out. It should remain on two hours, or until it dries and drops off. The same plaster, as big as a cent, applied to the hollow place under the ear, relieves the ear-ache. It may remain about an hour, and be succeeded by a little bat of cotton for a day after.

If a patient is too unconscious to complain, care should be taken to remove mustard applications in season. Bad blisters are sometimes produced by prolonging this powerful stimulus. If desirable to render it milder, it may be mixed with Indian meal.

OINTMENTS.

ALL rancid oils are inflaming ; therefore ointments should be made of very pure olive oil, fresh lard, or butter new and *unsalted* from the churn : the last is probably best. Sweet cream may be used, if unmixed with a particle of milk. The purity of olive oil, called sweet oil, is known by the absence of taste or smell.

The ingredients are usually simmered an hour or more, till they become crisped, or the color and qualities are obviously imparted. All leaves, stems, seeds, &c. should be separated by straining while warm.

Ointments should be kept covered from light and air. If they become rancid, they lose their healing properties.

House-Leek. (*Sempervivum Tectorum.*) The broken leaves, mixed with an equal portion of plantain, and slowly simmered in new butter, form an extremely cooling ointment for inflamed surfaces, blisters, &c.

Elder Bush, the leaf-buds, taken in early spring, and prepared in the same way, make a very soothing liniment. The inner bark of the bush is a useful ingredient to add to any cooling ointment.

Large White Garden Lily. (*Lilium Candidum.*) The bruised flowers form a healing ointment for external inflammations.

Hops made into ointment quiet the pain of cancerous sores, virulent eruptions, &c.

Mullein leaves, moistened in hot water, then simmered in fresh lard, form a soothing and quieting liniment.

Onions, sliced and simmered in lard, that has been previously melted and cooled five or six times, by being poured each time into a pailful of fresh water, make a salve highly praised for inflammation produced by taking cold in wounds.

Chalk, powdered and stirred into lard prepared by the same process, is very cooling to burns and inflammations.

Snow Ointment. Heat a little fresh lard till somewhat scorched. When cool, work in with a knife as much snow as it will take up. It is extremely cooling, and keeps pure a good while.

Cold Cream. Oil of almonds, two ounces; spermaceti, half an ounce; white wax half an ounce. Put them in a covered vessel, and place it in a skillet of boiling water. When melted, beat them up with a little rose-water till the whole becomes cold. Extremely soothing when the face and lips are inflamed by exposure to the wind; likewise comforting when soreness renders the act of nursing painful. It does not keep sweet longer than two or three weeks.

Simple Cerate. Fresh lard, six parts; white wax, three parts; spermaceti, one part. Slowly melted together, and stirred briskly till cold.

Spermaceti Ointment is prepared in the same way, with less oil and wax, and more spermaceti.

Basilicon Ointment. Fresh lard, eight parts; resin of pine, five parts; yellow wax, two parts. Melted and stirred.

Gall Ointment. Two drachms of finely powdered
12*

gall; half a drachm of fine opium, mixed with half an ounce of fresh lard. Good for piles. Applied after thorough washing with soft water. Equal portions of sulphur, cream of tartar, and powdered senna, one or two tea-spoonfuls daily, should be taken as a laxative.

Flour of Sulphur, one ounce thoroughly stirred in twice as much melted lard, and not strained, forms the common itch ointment. A little oil of lavender, or lemon, renders the odor less disagreeable. Rubbed in before a fire, several successive nights, and washed off with warm soap and water before a fresh application is made. A pound is enough for four unctions. If the whole body is infected, different portions should be anointed alternately, because it is unsafe to stop too many pores at once. Physic should be taken before it is applied. Flour of sulphur and cream of tartar, a tea-spoonful each, may be taken, night and morning, in a little molasses, or milk. The clothes worn during the infection ought to be smoked with brimstone and washed, lest they communicate the infection. People should be cautious not to mistake other eruptions for the itch, as great hazard might be incurred by suddenly striking them in.

It usually appears first on the wrists, or between the fingers, in the form of small watery bunches; but sometimes in large blotches, or white scurf. The neatest persons may take it by contagion, but perfect cleanliness will prevent its being severe.

*Poke Weed.** The purple berries should be crushed, squeezed through a cloth, and left in the air till the juice diminishes two thirds; then simmered with fresh lard. Used in some stages of salt-rheum, itch, and malignant ulcers. It has a somewhat caustic effect, tending to produce an eschar, or scabby covering.

---

* Likewise called garget, wild jalap, cocum, skoke, &c. *Phytolacca decandra.* It is quite a different plant from poke *root*, or American hellebore.

Bitter Sweet. An ointment of the leaves is very salutary for scrofulous and other humors.

Tobacco, half an ounce simmered in half a pound of lard makes a soothing ointment for irritable ulcers, scald-head, &c.

Apple of Peru. The seed vessels, or fresh leaves, well simmered in sweet lard, make a healing liniment, very highly recommended for scald-head, cutaneous eruptions, the piles, &c.

Charcoal pulverized, sifted, and thoroughly mixed with cold lard, arrests the progress of mortification, and is cleansing to putrid ulcers, scald-head, &c.

Tar, one ounce; flour of sulphur, half an ounce; fresh lard, two ounces; well mixed. Good for scald-head, and other ulcerous humors. It has peculiar facility in removing scabs and allaying itching. One third tar, simmered with two thirds pure mutton tallow, is recommended for salt-rheum. It should be removed daily with a sharp knife, and cleansed with a rag dipped in warm mutton tallow. The diet should be very low, and salts taken occasionally.

Broad-leaved Dock. The root made into an ointment and used perseveringly, has great reputation as a cure for cutaneous eruptions. A decoction of the root should be drank freely at the same time, and salts taken two or three times a week.

Smart Weed; Biting Knotweed; Water Pepper. (*Polygonum Hydropiper.*) Well known for the stinging acrimony of its taste. The bruised leaves made into an ointment, frequently and perseveringly applied, are highly recommended as a cure for cancers. This formidable disease might be often cured if it were attended to in season. A hard tumor, about the size of a hazle-nut, is usually the first symptom; and it sometimes remains unaltered for a very long time. As soon as it is discovered, ointments and poultices should be applied, purges taken twice or thrice a week, and all high-seasoned food, salt provisions, and stimulating liquors carefully avoided. Among various other causes, cancers are sometimes produced by the tight pressure of stays.

NARCOTIC POISONS.

Young persons should be cautioned against tasting of any roots, berries, seed, or leaves with which they are unacquainted. Many plants have narcotic qualities, like opium, producing distress, nausea, and giddiness, sometimes ending in convulsions and death. When people have been poisoned by swallowing *laudanum*, or similar substances, a thorough evacuation of the stomach is the first object. Powerful doses of emetic must be given instantly. Ipecac is recommended for narcotic poisons, because it peculiarly counteracts their effects. Thirty grains, mixed with the same quantity of sulphate of zinc, may be given to a grown person ; and fifteen grains of ipecac repeated every ten minutes, till it operates freely. If the wine of ipecac is used, half a gill may be given for the first dose, and a table-spoonful repeated. The inclination to vomit should be encouraged by tickling the throat with a feather, or with the finger, and by draughts of luke-warm water. If other emetics are not at hand, one table-spoonful of powdered mustard, stirred in a tumbler of warm water, and repeated if necessary, will generally induce vomiting. When the emetic has operated, a brisk dose of castor oil and jalap should be given. Olive oil in large quantities, broth, and gruel, are good, taken from time to time. Vinegar and lemon juice have been recommended ; but some physicians say they do much more harm than good. To counteract drowsiness, keep the patient walking, and give strong coffee, or strong green tea freely. A tea-spoonful of Water of Ammonia, (called Hartshorn,) in a wine-glass of water, every fifteen minutes, repeated for an hour or more, *if the emergency renders it necessary*, is said to have a very stimulating and rousing effect.

It should be persevered in, when the system seems sinking from reaction. If this cannot be obtained, a little clear brandy or rum may be given. At the same time, the body should be rubbed with salt, and hartshorn applied to the nostrils. The patient should not sleep for twelve hours. The diet should be very bland and simple during recovery.

MINERAL POISONS.

THE most common are *nitric acid*, *arsenic*, and *oxalic acid*. They produce burning heat in the mouth and stomach, acute pain, nausea, and hiccough. Repeated doses of calcined magnesia are the best antidote. If magnesia is not at hand, let a solution of soap and water be drank freely. It is made by dissolving half a pound of brown soap in a quart of water ; a cup-full should be given warm every three or four minutes. Chalk and water and lime-water likewise tend to neutralize the acid.

An emetic should be instantly given. Sulphate of zinc operates the quickest, and is always most safely administered mingled with ipecac. A grown person may take thirty grains of each in a glass of warm water ; and fifteen grains of ipecac may be repeated every ten minutes, if necessary. Assist the vomiting by copious draughts of warm barley-water, gruel, or flax-seed tea. Oils, and greasy substances increase the danger. Emollient fomentations and injections are useful. Physicians usually try bleeding, or leeches, when the inflammatory symptoms appear. During convalescence, the diet should be strictly confined to gruel, arrow-root, milk, &c.

When *corrosive sublimate* has been swallowed, the white of eggs, taken freely, will resolve it into a harmless mass.

Sugar, or syrup, in large quantities, is an antidote to the poison of *copper*, or *verdigris*.

Common salt is an antidote to *nitrate of silver*.

Sulphate of magnesia, or sulphate of soda, are good to counteract *sugar of lead* and other preparations of that metal.

When over doses of *tartar emetic*, or other *Antimonials* have been taken, yellow Peruvian bark will prevent the fatal effects. Quarter of a gill of the strong infusion is said to neutralize the effect of twenty grains of tartar-emetic. Almost any vegetable bitter will have the same effect ; therefore it is very improper to give chamomile tea, when you wish to vomit with *antimony*.

EXTERNAL POISON.

In many constitutions, a virulent and painful eruption is the consequence of merely handling such plants as the poison ivy, (*rhus radicans*,) and the dogwood, or poison sumach, (*rhus vernix*.) The first is a vine, with smooth, oval leaves, three clustering together at the end of a stalk ; flowers and berries small, and greenish white. The last is a shrub, with foliage resembling the locust tree, or common sumach. The young stalks tinged with fine red. Loose bunches of minute green flowers, and dry greenish berries.

Spots of the juice should be immediately wiped from the hands or clothes, and rubbed with chalk or magnesia, to prevent the infection's spreading. Cold water, or iced water, mitigates the burning sensation. Salt and water is perhaps still more cooling and efficacious. A solution of sugar of lead is often used as a wash. While these outward remedies are applied, the system must be kept thoroughly purged with salts, the diet must be very low, and all heating exercise avoided. Bleeding is generally recommended to plethoric persons.

People in the country highly praise a decoction of sweet fern, (*comptonia asplenifolia,*) both as a drink and a wash for external poison.

BATHS, AND FOMENTATIONS.

Dr. Dewees says, "Both the *hot* and *cold* baths are remedies of great power, and should never be used without the advice of a physician. The indiscriminate use of both has done more injury, we fear, than can ever be compensated by the good derived from their proper application." He defines the cold bath as one that produces a shock when applied to the human body. This effect is generally produced by water at sixty-two degrees, Fahrenheit's thermometer, especially in the form of a shower-bath. From eighty-two degrees to ninety-eight is the temperature of a *warm*, or *tepid*, bath. Above ninety-eight it is a hot bath.

It is a popular opinion that cold baths must be bracing; but, in fact, warm baths under some circumstances, produce this effect much better than cold ones. All tepid baths should be taken in a moderately warm room ; the towels for wiping should be warm and dry, and great care taken to cover the patient as soon as he is lifted from the water.

Very cold water is strengthening to weak backs, applied freely with a sponge *early in the morning*. Circumstances periodically occur which renders a cessation of the practice prudent for a few days.

A bath of luke-warm sea-water, for ten or fifteen minutes, every day, is much recommended for scrofulous complaints. A pretty good substitute can be made by dissolving salt in water.

A good vapor-bath can be prepared by placing *strong* sticks across a tub filled with scalding hot water. Let the patient sit upon them with every part of the person

entirely enveloped in blankets. When there is full
perspiration, place him in a very warm bed. This is
very beneficial in case of severe colds, violent colic,
&c. Bitter herbs are often steeped in the water, such
as tansy, wormwood, chamomile, &c. These are particularly useful when the steam-bath is used as an emmenagogue. If the herbs cannot be obtained, their
essence can be used instead. Sometimes bitter herbs
are applied to the bowels in bags moistened with hot
rum, or water, and frequently changed. Every precaution should be taken against admitting air into the
bed, and to prevent the danger of taking cold the following day.

When the patient is too weak to be raised up, a bath
may be given by placing a board on each side under
the bed-clothes ; at the foot of the bed, two other
narrow boards may descend into a tub filled with boiling
water, and completely enveloped in blankets, so that all
the steam may go up into the bed. It is well to place
very hot stones in the water, to preserve the heat. In
burning fevers, boughs of the hemlock tree (known for
its use in tanning) are thought to have a very quieting
effect, steeped in the water.

When the feet are soaked it should be in water as
warm as can be conveniently borne by the feet. If an
invalid cannot rise, fomentations may be applied as
follows :—When he is gone to bed, double a thick
blanket four square, put it between the sheets at the
bottom of the bed, and place his feet in the middle of it.
Have ready a gallon of water as hot as the hand can
endure ; put into it four towels ; wring two of these
dry, and apply them very hot, one to each ancle and
foot ; cover the feet well with the blanket and bed-
clothes. Every five minutes change the towels for hot
ones wrung dry from the water ; insinuate them very
carefully between the bed-clothes, so as not to admit
the air. Continue this process for half an hour, then
substitute hot *dry* towels ; place a hot brick at the feet,

let the doubled blanket remain as it is, and tuck up the foot of the bed, warm for the night.

If the patient is very chilly, hot cloths may be applied to the knees at the same time with the feet; taking very great care not to admit air into the bed. The arms should be kept in bed. Perspiration may be encouraged by warm diaphoretic drinks.

A table-spoonful of powdered mustard, or half a pint of vinegar, or a few spoonfuls of salt in a gallon of water prepared for the feet, tends to draw the blood from the head and body into the extremities. When there is violent pain in the head, it is sometimes a relief to apply cloths wet with cold water to the forehead, at the same time that hot ones are applied to the feet.

All fomentations should be much hotter than baths. Those applied for palsy, epilepsy, &c. are sometimes so hot as to be wrung with difficulty. In such cases, it is a good plan to make wide hems on the edges, and run strong sticks through them to assist the operation.

ENEMAS, OR INJECTIONS.

THE best instrument for this purpose is an accurate metallic syringe. If this cannot be obtained, its place may be imperfectly supplied by a bladder fastened very securely around an ivory pipe, or a piece of quill, or, in case of great soreness, a pliable India-rubber pipe; the liquid is forced upward by gradually compressing the bladder.

Fresh lard, or sweet oil should be put upon the pipe before it is applied, and the finger of the operator, well oiled, introduced into the passage, in order to ascertain its direction, and assist in the introduction of the pipe. For want of this last simple precaution, the instrument has sometimes been thrust through a child's intestines, and thus occasioned inflammation and death. The

13

operation is most conveniently performed when the patient is lying on his side, with the knees drawn up to the stomach, and a folded cloth placed under the hips to protect the bed-clothes. The luke-warm liquid should be injected slowly and gradually, and the hand not drawn backward after the process is begun.

These remedies are generally employed when the stomach rejects medicines, or is insensible to their impression ; but sometimes they are merely employed to assist the operation of medicines.

It takes twice as much of any medicine to produce an effect in this way, as when taken into the stomach ; but this should be applied with caution, because it varies in individuals. Very active remedies had always better be administered in less than stated proportions. When the object is to evacuate the bowels, from half a pint to a pint may be used for adults ; half that quantity for a child of eight or ten years old ; and from a quarter of a gill to two thirds of a gill, for an infant, according to age. Tobacco should never be given as an injection by the nurse.

When it is desirable to have the enema retained some time, or from weakness it refuses to do so, the materials should be very mild, and used in as *small quantities* as consist with convenience. The best materials are a warm solution of starch, or arrow-root; slippery elm tea ; flax-seed tea, boiled instead of steeped; even simple warm water does some good. In such cases, the quantity should seldom exceed half or two thirds of a gill. The patient should be induced to make an effort to retain it, and should be assisted, if necessary, by the pressure of a warm folded cloth.

In stranguary, occasioned by blister,—obstinate vomiting,—painful affections of the kidney and bladder, —cramp in the stomach,—or when drowsiness is desirable, and the stomach rejects opium,—about sixty drops of laudanum are added to half a pint of flax-seed tea, used as an injection, and retained two or three hours. Sometimes a few poppy blossoms are boiled with the flax-seed, to produce a quieting effect, instead of laudanum.

The following is a cathartic enema:—Two gills and a half of chamomile tea, steeped with carroway or fennel seed ; one ounce of olive oil ; one ounce of manna ; half an ounce of sulphate of magnesia ; well dissolved.

A more convenient kind, as good as the above, is made of one pint of warm water ; a table-spoonful of common salt ; two ditto of molasses ; and two of sweet oil, or fresh lard.

A very common one is made with half a pint of starch, of the common consistence, mixed with two great spoonfuls of linseed oil.

In cases of hysteric paroxysms, and other convulsions, assafœtida is sometimes administered ; two drachms in half a pint of warm water, gradually added and mixed ; from half a gill to a gill injected at once. Its laxative tendency is generally good ; but in some cases needs to be counteracted by the addition of a little laudanum.

Peruvian bark is sometimes used as an astringent ingredient in enemas, to check excessive purging.

Vinegar and water is used as an antiseptic injection in putrid disorders.

The following is one of the very best remedies for the piles :—An ounce of low mallows boiled in a pint of new milk, till reduced to three gills ; strain it, and add one gill of W. I. molasses. To be used about blood-warm ; injected daily.

There are India-rubber pipes so constructed that an invalid can administer injections to himself without any assistance.

The uterine syringe is applicable only to diseases of women. Its use can be easily ascertained by inquiring of nurses.

BLISTERS.

THE common blistering plaster is made of fresh mutton tallow, yellow wax, resin of pine, and cantharides, or Spanish flies ; equal portions of each. The flies are finely powdered and added to the other ingredients previously melted together and removed from the fire. Usually spread on soft leather or kid, somewhat larger than the hand. If the surface be spread with powdered flies, it is more irritating. If this fails to draw a blister, Venice turpentine, powdered mustard, and black pepper are sometimes mixed with it.

In common cases, a blister may remain from twelve to twenty-four hours, unless it produces stranguary ; then it should be immediately removed. If it sticks firmly, do not use force ; sponge it with warm water, and it will soon come away. If the little bladders are not already broken, snip them with sharp scissors, and apply a soft linen cloth, three or four times double, to absorb the discharge. Break the raised skin as little as possible. Dress it with a linen rag, well covered with spermaceti ointment, simple cerate, or basilicon ointment. Repeat this twice a day at first, and afterward daily till it is healed.

Cabbage leaves, or plantain, are often used as a soothing dressing. The stems should be cut out, and the rough inequalities bruised with a rolling-pin ; the leaves applied slightly warm, and the smooth side toward the blister. Sometimes they are moistened in warm milk, or spread with houseleek ointment, or some other cooling application.

If the blister becomes inflamed, make a poultice by stirring rye flour into boiling milk ; apply it luke-warm, its surface spread with *fresh* cooling ointment, or *pure* oil. It should be renewed three times a day ; and leaves as often.

A blistering plaster for young children had better be

sprinkled with a little powdered camphor on the surface before they are applied. When it has been on two hours, raise the edge, and see if the skin is deep cherry red; if so, take it off, and dress it with a rag covered with yellow basilicon. It will generally fill soon ; but if an hour after you see the color of the skin has faded, and it is not going to rise, apply the blister again for an hour or two ; when small blisters form here and there, it may be taken off, and the basilicon again put on for twenty-four hours ; after that, it may be dressed with bees-wax and sweet oil, or cold cream. By this process, stranguary is prevented, and you form an efficacious blister, that heals easily.

Cantharides are very apt to produce stranguary. This is said to be prevented by rubbing the part to be blistered with camphorated spirit before they are applied. When this difficulty has taken place, the dressings are sometimes strewed with very finely powdered camphor. The patient should drink freely of warm flax-seed tea ; and if the pain continue, a little gin may be added. A poultice of garlick, applied below the bowels, is good for stranguary ; so are sliced onions softened in boiling water, and put on in a thin muslin bag ; the same is said of small bags of salt, thoroughly warmed and frequently renewed.*

Sometimes, as a remedy for chronic diseases of the joints, &c., blisters are dressed with savin cerate, with the view of keeping them open, to promote continual discharge. A kind is made from the common red cedar that answers all the purpose. Of the fresh leaves, bruised, two pounds ; yellow wax one pound ; fresh lard four pounds. Melt the lard and wax together ; put the leaves in before it is hot; let them boil till they become crisp ; strain through a coarse cloth. Applied twice a day. Under its operation the discharge is apt to concrete on the surface of the blister, and needs to

* See injection of laudanum page 138.

be cleared away by the gentle pressure of an old linen cloth; sometimes a soft moist sponge may be used, if applied with great tenderness.

LEECHES.

THESE useful little worms are employed as the least painful means of drawing blood, and the most convenient to be applied to inflamed parts too tender for the lancet. Before they are put on, the part should be well cleansed with soap and water, and afterward with water; the hair, if there is any, should be cut off. In order to make them take hold where you wish, cut small holes in a piece of blotting-paper, lay it upon the place, and hold the vial of leeches up to it. If they do not bite readily, moisten the skin with a little blood, or milk and water. They continue to draw till they are full, and then drop off. If you wish to remove them sooner, sprinkle a little salt on them and they will fall. The bleeding may be encouraged as long as necessary with a sponge and warm water; when it is sufficient, squeeze the sponge dry, and repeatedly wipe the bitten places with it.

As a general rule, two leeches are applied when they wish to draw a fluid ounce of blood; but the number varies according to the part to which they are applied, and the degree of inflammation existing. A bite that would discharge one ounce of blood in a grown person, would discharge twice that quantity in a child. As young children do not bear leeching so well as other remedies in proportion to adults, it is often much better for them, in critical cases, to have the lancet applied by a physician; because in this way it is easy to know precisely how much blood is drawn.

American leeches do not make so deep an incision as the European, and draw less blood. Applied by inexperienced hands, they sometimes bite the arteries, or veins, and the risk may be great. In common cases, lint, or the nap of a hat, will usually be sufficient to stop the bleeding ; if not, apply a bunch of thin shavings of sole-leather, held on tight for half an hour.

If it continues to flow to an alarming degree, roll up a little cotton, or lint, or hat fur, into a hard ball about as big as small shot, and push it with a knitting-needle, or bodkin, into the hole made by the leech, so as to fill up the cavity. Then cover it with dry powdered plaster of Paris; the blood will soon moisten it, and it will form a hard surface to check the flowing. If it cannot be obtained, powdered alum, or burnt alum, will answer.

All these things may sometimes fail ; but bleeding may *always* be stopped by the following method :— Pinch up the skin at the puncture, so as to get good hold ; push a fine needle through the skin, so that the hole occasioned by the bite will come in the middle of the needle, and about one quarter of an inch of the skin will be taken up on each side ; then pat it down till the skin lies flat ; wind a strong thread round the needle, in and out like the figure 8 ; draw the thread tight as you wind, and the blood will soon stop flowing. The needle may usually be removed in the course of twelve or twenty-four hours ; but if the jugular vein is wounded it had better remain some days. Any person of moderate firmness may perform this simple operation ; and no child ever need bleed to death from a leech-bite after this has been read.

When arteries on the temples are cut by a leech, blood may easily be stopped by pressing the point of the finger firmly upon the bite for half an hour ; the skull-bone makes good resistance, and all is soon well.

ISSUES.

THE best way to make an issue is to burn a
small quantity of fresh white ash bark till reduced to
ashes ; put it in a muslin bag about the size of a thimble ;
wet it with water, and bind it on the place ; keep it
moist for several days, till the spot becomes black and
inflamed at the edges ; then apply warm Indian meal
poultices two or three times a day, till the blackened
part separates and comes out; into the hole thus made
insert a smooth, round piece of wax, about as big as a
pea ; place a piece of oiled silk, or very thin birch
bark, over it, and fasten it with a bandage.   It is very
necessary that the issue should be well cleansed with
luke-warm soap and water, the oiled silk sponged, and
a clean bandage renewed every day ; otherwise it will
become offensive.

Issues were formerly common as a drain for inveterate humors.   If the eruption appeared on the face
or neck, they were usually made on the fleshy part of
the arm ; if lower on the body, they were placed on
the inside of the leg, just below the knee.

They are usually kept open six months or a year.
They are dried up by simply taking the wax out, and
letting them heal ; when this is done, it is advisable to
take physic occasionally for a few weeks after.   Feeble
constitutions are sometimes weakened by them.   When
this effect is perceived, they should be dried up.

COMMON REMEDIES.

SOAK the feet in warm water ; bind upon them sliced
onions well heated ; take half a pint of strong pennyroyal, or calamint tea, at night; have your bed thoroughly
warmed ; and you will be almost sure to cure a cold,

if taken in season. Keep in the house the next day, and avoid currents of air.

A decoction of Irish moss, sweetened with honey, or W. I. molasses, is excellent for a cough. Molasses candy with this moss, or very thick flax-seed tea boiled in it, is likewise beneficial.

A table-spoonful of the brine in which rennet is preserved is extremely salutary in cases of indigestion and an acid stomach. A little water renders it less disagreeable, but it is better to take it clear.

A good quantity of *very old* cheese is an approved remedy when the stomach is oppressed with too much fruit, or other food. Half a tea-spoonful, or more, of pearl-ash dissolved in a little cold water affords relief under similar circumstances ; particularly if fat substances have been eaten.

A tea-spoonful of common ashes stirred in two large spoonfuls of boiling water, a tea-spoonful of it repeated at intervals, checks excessive vomiting and nausea. Some prefer to stir it in cider. It is often given in cases of cholera morbus.

A burning brand suddenly quenched, wrapped in flannel, and applied to the bowels is a most excellent application in case of violent colic. It retains its heat for a remarkable length of time, and sends forth a powerful steam, that produces perspiration.

O'Meara, surgeon to Napoleon, declares that a tea-spoonful of salt, moistened and put upon the tongue of a patient, during an epileptic fit, affords immediate relief.

When a limb is bruised by the fall of a window, or any other sudden weight, relief will be obtained by immediately placing it in quite warm water, and letting it remain fifteen minutes.

The odor of burning feathers, horn, or leather, is good for hysteric fainting fits.

A small lump of salt-petre dissolved in the mouth is good for common sore throats. When flannel is removed from the throat, bathe it in cold water, wear a thinner flannel for one day, then bathe it again, and there will be no danger of taking cold.

It is a very speedy cure for the itch, to stand half an hour, or more, in a tight barrel, covered to the throat with old blankets, or carpets; two or three lighted brimstone matches should be placed inside the barrel, by means of a small hole near the bottom, and every crevice stopped, that no smoke may escape. It is well to take moderate doses of sulphur, night and morning, for some days after.

A little pearl-ash and water, lime-water, or calcined magnesia, usually cures the hiccough.

A tea-spoonful of pearl-ash, in a pint of luke-warm water, forms a cooling wash for inflamed erysipelas.

Lamp oil is very healing to chapped hands. When applied, old gloves should be worn during the night.

The skin between the shell and the white of an egg is a cure for felons. It draws powerfully and increases the sharp pain, but affords relief in half an hour. The egg should be fresh, and the inner part of the skin placed next the flesh. The white of egg mixed with honey is said to be good for whitlows and felons.

Common clay moistened with water forms one of the best healing plasters to apply to stings. A slice of raw onion is likewise good; or salt moistened with water; or chalk wet with hartshorn.

The thin skin that comes from suet is good to bind upon the feet for chilblains. Rubbing them with spirits of turpentine, or Castile soap and honey, frequently and perseveringly, is much recommended. A wash made of chamomile flowers and poppy seed-vessels is useful; to be followed by the application of cooling ointments. Sometimes it becomes necessary to apply leeches to chilblains, and take active physic.

When the heels have been frost-bitten, take out the frost by immersion in snow, or cold water, and whenever they itch or burn, apply a rag well covered with hard soap and moistened with water.

A plaster made of equal parts of gum galbanum,

saffron, and camphor, is highly recommended for corns.
Very easy shoes should be worn, and the feet frequently bathed in luke-warm water, with a little salt and potash dissolved in it.

A shaving of hard soap will generally draw out a
corn in the course of six or eight days. It should be
bound on with a rag, changed every day, and the loose
skin lightly scraped off.

Pills made of old soap are a safe and good remedy
for the jaundice. Castile is generally preferred.
Three or four may be taken in the course of the day.

In asthma, it is a great relief to place the feet, knees,
and elbows, pretty deep in warm water. The patient
should be carefully guarded from taking cold.

To prevent the bones from pricking through the skin,
in the last stages of consumption, beat up the white of
an egg in two tea-spoonfuls of gin, and apply it spread
on old linen.

Cotton wool, wet with sweet oil and paregoric, relieves the ear-ache. A small tapering wedge of salt
pork, toasted a little, and put into the ear as far as convenient, has a similar effect; this has been known to
cure some kinds of deafness.

The ear-ache that follows measles is soon relieved by
filling the ear with quite hot milk. In a few minutes it
may be allowed to run out, and be filled again. The
ear should be covered with batted cotton four or five
days. Sometimes laudanum is added to the milk, in
the proportion of a tea-spoonful to a gill.

It is always well to bind a rind of pork, or spirits of
turpentine upon any wound occasioned by a needle, pin,
or nail, to *prevent* lock-jaw. If spasms indicate its
approach, bathe the scratch or wound freely with warm
weak lye, or pearl-ash and water, and send for a physician. Strong soft soap, mixed with powdered chalk,
applied in thin bags, is good for this dangerous disorder;
it should be kept moist till the wound begins to discharge, when the patient will find relief. The lock-
jaw has sometimes been cured by throwing tobacco

smoke into the mouth, so as to occasion distressing nausea.

Tobacco kept moist is an excellent application for a fresh cut or bruise. When the soreness is gone, cover the wound with court-plaster till it heals. Molasses, or salt, are good to bind on a fresh cut ; spirits of turpentine still better. Copal varnish relieves the soreness, and stops the flowing of blood.

It is a good sign for wounds to bleed freely ; but when this becomes very excessive, it may usually be stopped by the application of sole-leather scraped like coarse lint. Hartshorn or camphor should be in readiness to apply to the nose, as the stoppage of blood often induces faintness.

Inflammation may be drawn from a common burn by holding it resolutely near the fire, or in warm water. Raw potatoes scraped, afford relief. Four ounces of chloride of soda dissolved and stirred in a pint of water is a good wash for burns and scalds ; to be followed by cooling ointments. When a burn-blister breaks, it is said to be a good plan to sprinkle wheat flour on the naked flesh.

A small tea-spoonful of Water of Ammonia (called Hartshorn) swallowed in a wine-glass of water, every fifteen minutes, for an hour or more, is considered a specific for the bite of a rattle-snake ; at the same time the wound should be very frequently washed in the same preparation, somewhat stronger, and the blood repeatedly squeezed out, as long as a drop can be obtained. Ammonia in large quantities is poison ; but its effects may be counteracted by lemon juice, vinegar, &c.

Note. Page 45, it is stated that when laudanum is used for injections, doses may be safely increased three or four fold. This is Dr. Dewees's opinion; but some physicians consider it unsafe in such quantities, until its effect on the constitution has been fairly tested. Page 30, cream of tartar is said to be good for fevers; it should have been added, " when not attended with diarrhea." Page 31, there should have been a caution to omit molasses and lemon in toast and water when diarrhea is present.

EXPLANATION OF TERMS.

Acrid—sharp and biting to the taste.
Anodyne—assuaging pain ; quieting.
Anthelmintic—that which kills worms.
Antiseptic—antiputrescent, or counteracting putrefaction ; preventing mortification.
Antispasmodic—relieving cramp and nervous spasms.
Aperient—slightly laxative.
Aqueous—watery.
Aromatic—fragrant ; spicy ; warming and stimulating.
Asthma—wheezing cough ; difficulty of breathing.
Astringent—binding ; contracting ; opposite to laxative.
Calculous—relating to stones and gravel.
Carminative—that which expels wind.
Cathartic—purging ; operating as physic.
Catarrh—a disease producing frequent discharges from the nose.
Caustic—burning ; drying up humors ; producing a scabby covering.
Chronic—of long duration ; habitual.
Coagulum—a clot of milk, or blood, &c.
Constipating—astringent ; binding.
Contagious—communicated by touch, or by close vicinity.
Cutaneous—relating to the skin.
Demulcent—softening ; soothing irritation.
Diaphoretic—producing perspiration.
Diarrhea—severe form of dysentery.
Diuretic—promoting discharge of urine.
Dyspepsia—distress occasioned by indigestion of food.

14

Emetic—occasioning vomiting, or puking.

Emmenagogue—that which promotes a periodical discharge, when it is obstructed in women by colds, or sedentary employments.

Emollient—softening ; soothing.

Epidemic—applied to a disease when general, and supposed to be in the air.

Erysipelas—a fiery eruption called St. Anthony's fire.

Expectorant—promoting a discharge of phlegm from the lungs.

Farinaceous—mealy ; containing flour.

Fetid—having an offensive smell.

Flatulence—windiness.

Fluor Albus—a white discharge producing female weakness.

Fomentations—warm liquors applied with cloths.

Hemorrhage—bleeding from the lungs, broken blood-vessels, &c.

Laxative—gently purgative.

Mucilaginous—slimy ; ropy ; mucous.

Narcotic—causing sleep, or stupor.

Nausea—slight sickness at the stomach.

Pectoral—relating to diseases of the chest.

Perennial—lasting year after year.

Phlegmatic—sluggish ; not easily excited.

Plethoric—full of blood.

Pleurisy—disease of the chest, attendant on consumption.

Pulmonary—relating to the lungs.

Pulverized—reduced to powder.

Purgative—cathartic ; purging the bowels.

Refrigerant—cooling.

Rubefacient—making the skin red and burning.

Saline—consisting of salts.

Scorbutic—relating to the scurvy.

Spasmodic—consisting of spasms, or convulsed motions.

Specific—a certain cure.

Stomachic—strengthening to the stomach.
Sudorific—producing perspiration in a great degree.
Suporific—producing drowsiness.
Suppository—a long round substance, like a pipe-stem.
Suppurative—ripening; bringing to a head.
Tonic—gradually strengthening the whole system.
Tumor—a swelling.
Uterine—relating to the womb, and organs connected therewith.
Vaccination—inoculation with kine-pox, or cow-pox.

ALPHABETICAL INDEX.